encaustic WORKSHOP

Artistic Techniques for Working with Wax

PATRICIA BALDWIN SEGGEBRUCH

NORTH LIGHT BOOKS
Cincinnati, Ohio
www.mycraftivity.com

Encaustic Workshop

13 12 11 10   5 4 3

Distributed in Canada by Fraser Direct
100 Armstrong Avenue
Georgetown, ON, Canada L7G 5S4
Tel: (905) 877-4411

Distributed in the U.K. and Europe by David & Charles
Brunel House, Newton Abbot, Devon, TQ12 4PU, England
Tel: (+44) 1626 323200, Fax: (+44) 1626 323319
E-mail: postmaster@davidandcharles.co.uk

Distributed in Australia by Capricorn Link
P.O. Box 704, S. Windsor, NSW 2756 Australia
Tel: (02) 4577-3555

Library of Congress Cataloging-in-Publication Data

Seggebruch, Patricia Baldwin.
  Encaustic workshop : artistic techniques for working with wax / Patricia Seggebruch. -- 1st ed.
     p. cm.
  Includes index.
  ISBN 978-1-60061-106-3 (pbk. : alk. paper)
  1. Wax craft. 2. Encaustic painting. I. Title.
  TT866.S45 2009
  736'.93--dc22

                    2008025927

www.fwpublications.com

Editors: Tonia Davenport and Jessica Strawser
Designer: Marissa Bowers
Production Coordinator: Greg Nock
Photographers: Adam Hand, Christine Polomsky
            and Bethany Vail

DEDICATION

"My business is not to remake myself,
But make the absolute best of what God made." **—Robert Browning**

I believe part of my business is to share with enthusiasm and passion the things I've come to learn and discover on earth. Therefore, it is my hope that this book carries the absolute best of me and that some of the passion I carry for this medium will be passed to you. And so, this book is first and foremost dedicated to you, my readers!

To the best four redheads in the whole wide world—Conner, Daniel, Brian and Patrick—who continue to believe that having an artist for a mom is a cool thing.

To mom and dad: For allowing me to doodle on surfaces not always designed for such creative expression.

To my painting pals: Loving support is a gift and a blessing!

To John: Love unconditionally. Life is too short.

ACKNOWLEDGMENTS

Without the support and encouragement from Ampersand Art Supply, Daniel Smith Finest Quality Artists' Materials and R&F Handmade Paints, the energy behind this book would never have been ignited. Deepest thanks to them all for their generous and heartfelt support.

Thanks also to North Light Books and the team who brought this unknown, untrod path of publication to light for me. So much joy in a dream realized!

 contents

Waxing
POETIC

The beauty of art: Isn't that what's drawn you to this book, to this medium, to painting at all? The splendor of it? The simple pleasure of looking at a beautiful painting and feeling your heart respond, your soul wake up? Not your mind—it's been working on overtime with life's tasks—but your heart and soul.

So it was for me upon discovering the joy of encaustic. It is where I found, and continue to find, my closest connection to the world at large—and to the smaller one on the inside. This medium is a dynamic one where anything goes and the possibilities are endless. If you are seeking creative release and experimentation, you will find it in this medium.

Encaustic literally means "to burn." In its most basic interpretation, then, encaustic is hot, melted (or burned, if you will) wax. It can be as simple as beeswax melted and applied to an absorbent surface. Ancient beginnings harken back to Trojan ships sealed with pigmented wax; the original intent to make them watertight evolved into a means of decorating and personalizing each ship. The modern-day revival of encaustic and the experimental anything-goes nature of today's art world have allowed for a tremendous resurgence of painting in hot wax, experimenting with any and all techniques in it.

My goal is to bring the encaustic workshop to you in your own studio as I walk you through each step in creating beautiful encaustic paintings. If this is your first taste of encaustic, begin with the simple application of wax to the board. Then, once you're comfortable with the basics, begin exploring all the possibilities in the medium, step by step. Delve into incising (see page 28), try your hand at collage (see page 38) or jump into image transfers (see page 58). Each chapter provides new techniques that will further enrich and enliven your encaustic painting and your own enjoyment of working in this versatile medium.

If you have experience with encaustic and have come to this book with the hope of finding new and exciting techniques to enhance your work, skip to the chapter headings and pick one to inspire you to fresh approaches to the medium. Then, try them all. Play, experiment and discover the rich, organic nature of the medium.

And, as I do in all my workshops, I invite you to keep in touch. Feel free to ask me the question that's got you puzzled or simply to share your experiences in encaustic with me by visiting www.pbsartist.com.

At the end of all the toe-tapping, blood-pumping fun technique chapters in this book, I've included an Inspiration Gallery filled with examples of my paintings that combine the techniques outlined in this book in new and interesting ways. I hope it shows you that this is just the beginning of what you can accomplish in encaustic! And remember, creativity happens in the pauses; pause, take a deep breath and turn the page. Let's begin!

> "You agree—
> I'm sure you agree,
> that beauty is
> the only thing
> worth living for."
>
> **Agatha Christie**

TOOLS AND MATERIALS

Oftentimes artists will shy away from beginning in encaustic because they fear a costly investment to get started or a messy setup that will take over their studios. Neither fear is warranted. The cost can be kept minimal by investing in hardware products from home stores or hardware stores (which work just as well as more specialized products), and the mess is nonexistent. The product is self-contained in its cooled state, and all tools and surfaces can be cleaned by simply melting the wax away. In fact, if you're using brushes and other tools specifically for this medium, they need not be cleaned at all!

You need only a few basic essentials to begin encaustic painting. I've listed them here, along with a few of my favorite tools, to get you started. As you begin to explore the techniques in this book you will realize that the possibilities for tools and materials compatible with encaustic are endless. Anything goes! Once you master working with the basic elements of the medium, the sky is the limit.

WAX

Refined beeswax is the standard in encaustic painting. It has been treated to remove the natural yellow of the beeswax. It produces a clear, glass-like painting when used with or without damar resin. Refined is a better choice than bleached beeswax as the bleached wax can yellow over time due to the chemical processing it's gone through.

Natural beeswax is a gorgeous choice for rich, organic painting because it is still in its natural, yellow state, and it lends that quality to the finished work.

Here you can see the difference in appearance between natural beeswax, at the top, versus refined clear medium, shown just beneath it.

Damar resin can be added to the beeswax to add a bit of durability and luminosity to the encaustic painting. But this additive is not required, and some artists work strictly in beeswax and obtain durable, luminous results.

Medium is the name given to the combination of beeswax and damar resin. You can make your own, but premade medium is the most advantageous choice for ease of use. This is a combination of refined beeswax and damar resin that has been designated the optimal combination by the producer. All that is required of you is to melt it down and paint. The choice between refined beeswax, natural beeswax and medium is a personal one, and I encourage you to experiment with each to find your preference.

There are many sources for encaustic wax out there, from your local beekeeper producing natural wax to international companies creating beautiful refined waxes for clear, white application. I encourage you to explore your options, but if you are a beginner, I recommend using refined beeswax or medium from R&F Handmade Paints. R&F has been perfecting its products for decades and is dedicated to producing the best encaustic products for artists.

This, combined with the fact that its customer service representatives can answer any questions a beginning encaustic artist may have about product and technique, makes R&F a fabulous resource for all things hot wax.

PALETTE AND TINS

The palette in encaustic work is where the wax is melted, mixed with colored pigment and kept fluid. Any flat surface that can be heated will suffice as a palette, but it is important to have a regulated heat gauge, rather than one with simple "low, medium and high" settings, in order to control the wax temperature. The temperature of the palette needs to be around 220°F (104°C) to maintain an optimal melted wax temperature of 180°–220°F (82°–104°C).

Two great palette options are an anodized aluminum palette designed specifically for this purpose or a simple griddle from the small appliance section of any home store. The anodized aluminum palette is great for mixing colors directly on the surface, as it has a clear surface that maintains true color representations in mixing. But this surface does require a separate electric stove element placed underneath the palette to heat it. The griddle is not an advisable surface for directly mixing colors, but it is fairly inexpensive, has a nice, large surface area, and heats up evenly and automatically all on its own.

The cleanest and most efficient way to have multiple colors of wax melted at the ready at one time is to use tins arranged on the palette to hold different encaustic paints. I prefer 16-ounce (473ml) seamless printmakers' ink cans from Daniel Smith Art Materials, but anything similar would also work. I have found these cans to be indispensable in my encaustic setup because they allow for large volumes of wax to be always at the ready—and for my brushes

This typical palette setup features printmaking ink cans filled with colored wax and uses an anodized aluminum palette from R&F Handmade Paints; the palette thermometer helps monitor the wax temperature.

to remain upright in their designated cans. You can mix a different color in each one, and if you need just a small amount of a color, you can even use the lids to mix limited quantities.

The palette setup described here is wonderful for an easy cleanup; just turn everything off and let it cool down. When beginning again the next day, simply warm the palette: Wax melts, brushes loosen and painting can begin again.

When the wax is completely melted on the typical palette setup, simply assign a natural bristle brush to each color for easy painting and hassle-free cleanup.

FUSING TOOLS

Fusing is the reheating of each applied layer of wax so that it bonds with the preceding layer, thus ensuring a cohesive surface to your encaustic painting. The heat gun is my tool of choice for fusing because it offers control and ease of use. R&F sells a nice one, and others are available from other encaustic sources and hardware stores. I have a preference for the Wagner Heat Gun. It offers variable temperature control separate from a variable air flow control.

Alternative fusing tools are propane torches, irons and tacking irons. The propane torch offers a strong, concentrated flame and works well for spot fusing, but offers less control for fusing an entire surface. The iron and tacking iron both work well for either spot fusing or surface fusing, but I find less control with these tools than with the heat gun because the irons apply the heat directly to the wax. For this reason, they must be set at exactly the right heat setting so as not to melt any of the wax away from the surface.

SURFACES

Two rules here: rigid and absorbent. It is important that the surface on which you paint in encaustic is rigid, meaning it cannot be flexible. The wax cools hard and will chip off of a surface that has any give to it, such as paper or canvas. If you enjoy these surfaces, you can paint in encaustic on them as long as you first adhere them to a board support.

The surface also needs to be absorbent. The wax has to have something to grab hold of in order to establish a solid foundation on which to build with more wax and additional elements.

My favorite boards to use for encaustic are Ampersand's Claybords. They have a luminous white clay surface that receives wax beautifully and establishes a vibrant foundation for color. The board itself comes in a flat panel, ¾" (2cm) cradle or 2" (5cm) cradle. Encaustic is very conducive to the 2" (5cm) cradle as it allows for no framing and this contemporary look maximizes the finished encaustic product.

Birch plywood panels from the hardware store are great encaustic surfaces as well. They come in different widths, can be cut to any size you choose, and tend to be the most white of the natural board surfaces available. But any unfinished, untreated wood, such as plywood or even scrap wood, will work as a surface for encaustic painting.

BRUSHES

One rule: Go natural. Synthetic brushes will melt in the hot wax. My favorites, both from Daniel Smith Art Materials, are hog bristle brushes in assorted sizes and hake brushes (also known as sumi painting brushes). Avoid using brushes with nailed, metal handles, as the heating and cooling of the wax eventually loosens those nails and causes the bristles to fall out. Brushes ranging in size from 1"–3" (3cm–8cm) work well for all the techniques shown in this book.

OTHER TOOLS

I enjoy experimenting with anything that I think could have an interesting effect on the wax. For incising—or cutting design elements into the wax—I turn to pottery tools, awls, styluses, cookie cutters, hardware store putty knives and filing tools. From the scrapbooking stores I collect stamps, interesting stickers, embellishments and rub-ons. My favorite burnishing tool is a simple spoon, but bone folders and scissor handles work well, too. Other tools I have readily available for use in my encaustic studio are a metal ruler for straight line incising, a small propane torch, assorted screens and stencils for incising, and extension cords to allow for maximum reach with my heat gun.

MIXED MEDIA

Art supply and craft stores are great places to collect interesting collage papers, foils, leafing, oil paints, pastels, charcoals and photo transfer papers for use with the various encaustic techniques you will learn in this book. Likewise, scrapbooking stores offer a nice selection of rub-ons, papers, items to embed in your work and even unique incising tools.

I scour hardware stores, fabric stores, salvage yards, thrift shops and garage sales for interesting materials to use in my encaustic work. Look for one-of-a-kind items to embed, from vintage buttons to rusty coils. You may even be surprised by effective treasures found lingering in your junk drawer.

Leave no stone unturned in your search for innovative materials to use in your encaustic work. I can't begin to list them all, and I'm willing to bet that once you get started, you will find some I have yet to discover.

These hake, or sumi painting, brushes are my personal favorites for encaustic work, but any natural bristle brushes will do.

Color
IT UP

Without color, there is a limit to art—and encaustic is about creating without limits! There are several options available to mix colored beauty into plain beeswax. Each artist has his or her own level of interest, patience, skill and, yes, even time that will indicate which coloring option works best for him or her. The three explored here—pigmented medium, oil paint additive and dry pigment—are all viable and equally effective options. Pigmented waxes are my personal medium of choice; I find them easy to use and enjoy working with their reliable, consistant colors. But I encourage you to experiment with them all and determine your own personal favorite. There is no right or wrong method to choose.

"We can't take any credit for our talents. It's how we use them that counts."

Madeleine L'Engle

CREATING COLORED WAX

There are three main types of color you can add to your wax for your encaustic painting: pigmented medium, dry pigment additive and oil paint additive. All can be beautiful mediums for achieving colorful encaustic artwork.

PIGMENTED MEDIUM

This is my steadfast favorite option. Not only is it the easiest, neatest and safest, but the array of color options and consistency of color are an easy sell. These premade colors are sold through many encaustic producers, but I use R&F Handmade Paints in illustrating the techniques throughout this book. These encaustic paints come in rectangular blocks that fit nicely into the large printmakers cans from Daniel Smith Art Materials that I use for quick melting.

Encaustic manufacturers have machines that produce a beautiful color in the wax by milling the colors to a very fine consistency. Pigment suspension in the wax is optimal with these products. And their intensity can be varied simply by adding medium (see page 20).

PIGMENTED ADDITIVE

You can also make your own colored wax by adding dry pigments to medium to create customized colors. This method should be used with caution, as it involves working with loose particles that can be very dangerous to inhale. Also, getting a consistent color throughout a batch—or re-creating a color exactly as you created it before—can be difficult. I try to stay away from this technique because I favor the consistent hue and ease of use of the ready-made pigmented medium, but many artists find mixing their own encaustic paints satisfying.

Assorted blocks of premade pigmented medium, pictured with a larger block of clear medium, add vibrant, consistent color to encaustic work.

OIL ADDITIVE

A third choice for getting colored wax is to add oil paints or oil paint sticks to the medium. This, too, can be effective and enjoyable if you like to create your own colors. I have found that oil paint sticks work better than traditional oil paints because the greater oil content in the traditional paints can dilute the medium, but you can use either successfully by following the steps below.

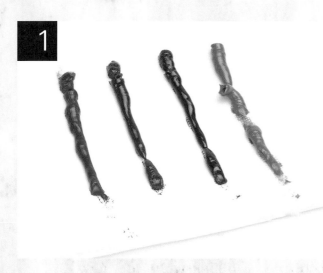

Oil paint sticks offer a simpler alternative to traditional oil paints.

1 Prepare oil paint overnight

Squeeze oil paint onto a paper towel and let it sit overnight so the excess oil leaches from the pigment. This will allow the pigment to blend more easily into the medium in step 2.

2 Add paint to melted medium

Add a bit of the paint directly to some hot wax medium. Experiment with the concentration— being conservative at first and gradually adding more—in order to achieve your desired intensity of color.

ANOTHER APPROACH

Opt for oil sticks

The oil content of oil sticks is much less than that of traditional oil paints, so they can be added directly to the medium without the paper towel leaching process in step 1. Simply cut them directly into the hot, melted wax medium. Here I am using an R&F Handmade Paints oil stick.

Ritratto d'un Asino ... — £ 5 10 —

Ritratto di ... — £ 4 4 —

Ritratto d'un ... — 25 5

Ritratto di un Montone ... — 1 — 5 — 5

ARE WE THERE YET?

Set
IT UP

The most basic technique one needs to learn when working in encaustic is how to work with the hot wax. In this medium the play of paint on the brush and how it can be applied works differently from other mediums. Because the wax is hot, and needs to remain so in order to continue to be workable, the brush must be returned to the paint pot at fairly regular intervals. The way you move the brush can also create varying applications of wax. You can alter your approach to create a simple priming layer, a thick or thin application of wax, a smooth finish or a highly textured surface. All will be explored in this chapter. The techniques demonstrated here should serve as a jumping-off point for all other encaustic techniques. Refer to these pages as often as you need to as you work your way through the many methods illustrated in this book.

> " I'm still learning
> that there are no mistakes,
> only discoveries. "
>
> **Fernando
> Ferreira
> De Araujo**

PRIMING AND FUSING

When beginning an encaustic painting, it is recommended that you prime the surface. This prepares the board to receive the colors optimally and ensures an even, smooth surface to begin work on. The application of wax to the board is an easy process. In the following steps you'll see just how simple it is; with a little practice, you'll master these methods in no time. Apply these techniques to several different boards to see firsthand how the wax reacts to each one. I use smooth Ampersand Claybord in all my encaustic work and all the examples in this book.

When priming, plain beeswax is the least costly option. Medium can be used just as effectively if that is all you have on hand, but since this layer will be covered by pigmented medium, plain medium or other elements, it is not necessary for this layer to have the luminosity provided by the damar resin in the medium.

Claybord or
plywood panel
melted beeswax
heat gun or fusing tool
of choice
wide paintbrush
(2 ½" [6cm] hake
recommended)
needle tool (optional)

1

Heat surface

Begin any painting with a smooth, glass-like surface, even if you will choose to paint texturally in the end. This keeps all your options open for future layers.

Heat the surface of the Claybord with a heat gun until it's just warm to the touch (about 30 seconds, depending on the size of the board). Be mindful to keep the gun moving in gentle, smooth motions across the entire surface; otherwise, you'll develop hot spots that will resist the wax application.

2

Apply the wax

Brush a thin layer of beeswax or medium in smooth, even strokes across the warm board. Try not to overlap the layers, as doing so can make fusing more difficult.

18

Fuse base layer

Fuse the entire piece by heating the surface with the heat gun until the finish turns from dull to shiny. This will suffice as a base for much encaustic work. If it's important for you to achieve a completely smooth primed surface, go a step further and overfuse the surface. To overfuse, simply heat the surface until the wax becomes fluid and visibly soaks into the board.

Re-fuse incomplete areas

If any areas are unwaxed after the first application, simply apply additional wax to those areas and re-fuse them with the heat gun.

Fix any final flaws

If you see any stray hairs or particles in the wax, gently pick them out with a needle tool. Reheat to smooth the disturbed wax.

brush up

When re-fusing a layer, keep the heat gun moving to avoid creating hot spots, which will appear as small craters.

VARYING THICKNESS

Varying degrees of color intensity are desired in the basic paint application in any medium. With encaustic it is easy to achieve different shades of color by simply adding medium to the color of choice. Here I'm using Quinacridone Magenta to illustrate the degrees of opacity and transparency achievable in this method.

WHAT YOU'LL NEED

primed board

encaustic paints in color(s) of your choosing

medium

heat gun or other fusing tool

paintbrushes of varying widths

tin lids or other palette for mixing paint

Prepare pigment
To change the intensity of the color, simply add varying amounts of the clear medium to the solid pigment. In this example I am beginning with straight pigmented wax with no additional medium. You can see that in its purest form, the color is very dense and opaque.

Paint surface
Brush the color onto the surface.

Add a bit of medium
Here I've added one part medium to the straight color, then brushed it onto the board. You can see it is thinner and slightly more transparent than the pure color brushed above it.

Experiment with mixing pigment and medium
The more medium you add, the more transparent the color. The final, most transparent application shown here was produced by mixing 1 part color to 3 parts medium.

VARIEGATED

The depth of color in this piece changes from the dense, flat opaque to the thin, transparent hint of color, creating a fading effect from top to bottom. Beyond more abstract work, varying opacity in this way can be used effectively for painting encaustic sunsets and landscapes.

ACHIEVING TEXTURE

Texture is what working with encaustic is all about. Whether you want to create a finish that's as smooth as glass or produce a deep, three-dimensional image, you can accomplish it with wax. On the following pages, I will show you the basic smooth application and the basic texture application. Then we'll experiment with adaptations of each throughout the rest of this book.

SMOOTH APPLICATION

Smooth layers varying in thickness can be used to create a finished look as well as to embed and layer images, papers, elements and words. Here you'll see the effects you can create by simply painting two layers of color and fusing between each application. Any number of layers can be applied to create varied effects. Just keep in mind that each layer needs to be fused before the next is added.

WHAT YOU'LL NEED

primed board

encaustic paint in
color of your choosing

heat gun or
other fusing tool

paintbrush

Apply color to warm surface
Begin this process with a warm board. Brush a fairly even layer of color over it, trying to not overlap the application too much. (An uneven layer of color can make the fusing process more difficult.)

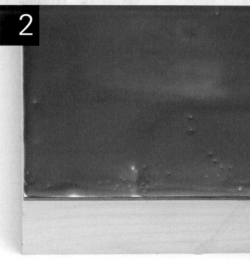

Fuse painted surface
Fuse the layer with a heat gun. You may see some uneven areas or even missing color; that's OK for now.

Apply a second layer and re-fuse
Brush on a second layer of color and fuse to create a consistent, solid layer of color. This second application often takes care of any unevenness or missed spots from the first layer.

TEXTURED APPLICATION

This technique can be used to add depth to any encaustic painting. At a less abstract level, it can be used to produce interesting foliage, branches, grass and landscaping details in realistic work. It can even be used with small hog bristle brushes to create beautiful, ethereal trees.

WHAT YOU'LL NEED

primed board

encaustic paints in colors of your choosing

heat gun or other fusing tool

brushes of varying sizes

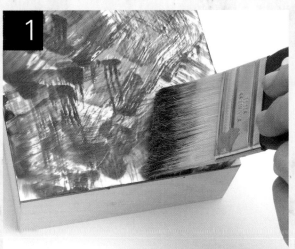

Apply color to cool board

Start with a cool, primed board. (If you start with a warm board, the texture you're able to create using this technique is more limited.) Using a dry, coarse brush (this one is made from hog bristle), apply color over the board, varying the directions of your brushstrokes.

Fuse, cool and apply second coat

Fuse the layer of color with a quick hit of the heat gun, just enough to change the appearance from dull to shiny. Let it cool completely. Apply a second color using the same dry-brush action as in the first application. Again, let the surface cool.

Layer colors and fuse

Continue applying layers of color, fusing and letting the board cool between each layer. I prefer to work my colors from light to dark, creating a "glow" of light color coming through the deeper color layers, but feel free to experiment with different effects.

Continue until texture is rich

Continue until you create a look you like. Here, I've used just five layers to create this beautifully rich and textured effect.

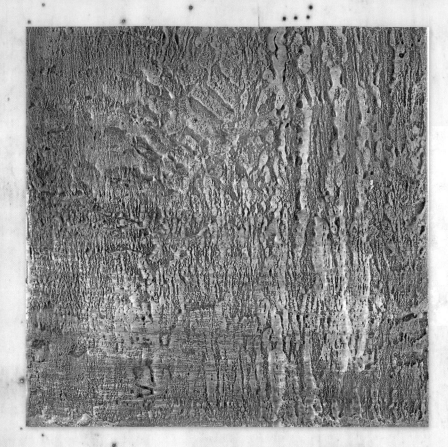

MINTY

This piece is another example of the visual and tactile texture that can be created using the textured application technique shown on the previous page.

PASTELS

This alternate example of the textured application shows how, by building layers in this manner, deep crevasses and thick hills can ultimately be created.

spOt on

SPOT ON

In contrast to the pieces on the opposite page, this encaustic collage is created by papers layered in the encaustic and covered with a thick, smooth application of medium using the technique described on page 22. (We'll learn more about encaustic collages starting on page 38.) Most of the pieces throughout this book exemplify the smooth application technique.

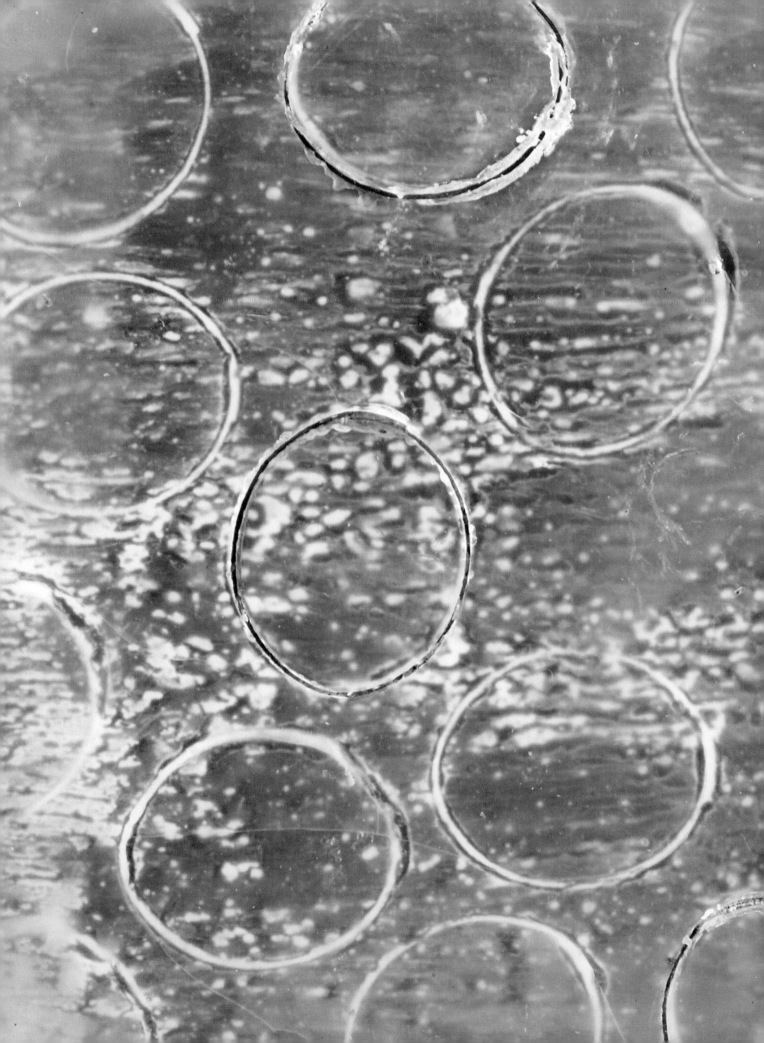

Cut
IT IN

The organic, pliable nature of beeswax can create an effect of depth that other mediums cannot. Incising, or cutting into, the wax can be done as simply as a thin straight line or as intricately as a detailed portrait. Glazing and filling the incising with paint, or even colored wax, enhances the cut lines and adds richness to the encaustic painting, whether used as a stand alone technique or incorporated into a painting in combination with other methods. On the following pages you'll learn techniques for incising with several different metal tools in fine lines as well as thick cuts. Then, you'll learn how to use metal stencils to add texture to your work. Finally, you'll see how layers of colored wax can be scraped away to achieve deep, rich effects unlike those created by any other medium.

> "A lot of it's experimental, spontaneous. It's about knocking about in the studio and bumping into things."
> **Richard Prince**

INCISING

Any metal tool that can be used to cut into the wax lends itself to this most versatile of techniques. Tools that I've tried with great success include awls, cookie cutters, styluses, razor blades, wire brushes, pottery tools, palette knives, metal combs and nails or screws. Look for inspiration in textures; find tools at craft stores, hobby shops, flea markets, salvage yards, pottery stores, hardware stores and just about anywhere else you can find interesting metal objects. I've even found one-of-a-kind objects along the side of the road on my morning walk that have become some of the best items for incising in my encaustic paintings. It is not imperative that you know exactly how the objects will incise the wax or precisely where they will be best used in the painting. It is much more satisfying to let the wax and incising tools inspire the painting as you begin using them together.

INCISING FINE LINES

Any metal tool with a sharp tip or a thin edge will incise the wax with fine lines that can be used to add detail or subtle texture and color to any work of encaustic art.

WHAT YOU'LL NEED

primed board

clear medium or encaustic paints in colors of your choosing

heat gun or other fusing tool

incising tool of your choosing (cookie cutter and wire brush shown here)

needle tool or pick

oil paints or oil paint sticks in colors of your choosing

rubber gloves

paper towels or shop towels

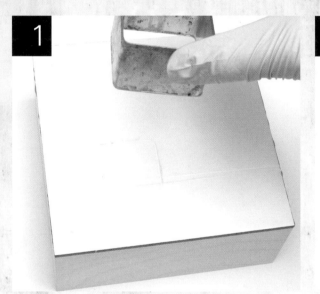

1

Layer wax and make impressions
Over a primed board, apply one or two layers of clear medium or colored wax; fuse after each layer. While the top layer is still warm, press shapes into the wax; here I'm using a cookie cutter.

2

Scrape lines into wax
To scrape lines into the surface, use a needle tool or pick. A metal straightedge can be used to create a straight line. For a more organic look, simply work freehand to create interesting, moving and flowing lines as well as straight ones.

brush up

Even if they're "clean," encaustic tools should remain exclusive to encaustic work to ensure no transferring of wax, particles or other materials between mediums, or heaven forbid, food!

Add additional texture with a wire brush

Experiment with using a wire brush in the wax to create incised texture. It is more effective to allow the wax to cool before beginning this particular incising technique, as the bristles are so compact they tend to make a gummy mess of warm wax.

Apply color to textured areas

After you have achieved the desired texture, let the wax cool. (Otherwise, you'll smush the wax in step 5.) Add some color with an oil paint stick or oil paint. I am using an R&F paint stick in Alizarin Crimson.

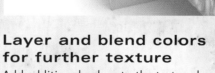

Work color into textured areas

Wearing gloves to protect your skin and to make for easy cleanup, rub the color into the board with your fingers.

Layer and blend colors for further texture

Add additional colors to the textured areas if you'd like, blending them directly on the board.

brush up

To easily remove the burrs created when scraping in line work, let the medium cool and then just brush them loose.

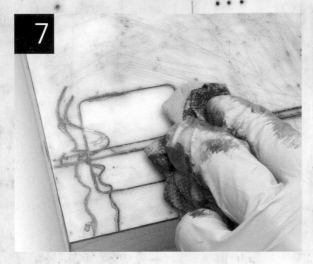

Remove excess

After blending in the desired colors, wipe off the excess with a shop towel or paper towel. Be sure to remove as much of the excess color as you can. If too much oil paint/stick is left on the wax, there is a tendency for the wax to resist adhesion to the subsequent layers, and you'll have sliding artwork.

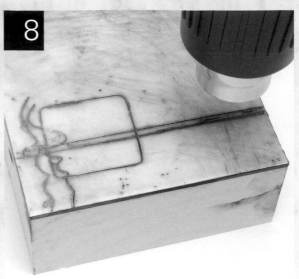

Fuse surface

Even though this is not an additional wax layer, the incised area is an added layer and needs to be fused. A quick fuse is sufficient.

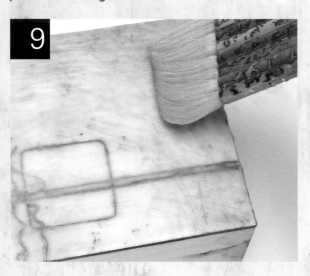

Layer medium and fuse again

Brush on a layer or two of medium, fusing between layers. Don't worry about leaving brushstokes, as this can add more incising texture.

Glaze with color

Apply a new layer of glaze (here I'm using oil paint sticks) over the fused medium, working the color over the textured areas that were incised by the brushstrokes in the last step.

Wipe and fuse

Again, wipe off the excess color. Fuse the new layer a final time to complete the piece.

INCISING THICK LINES

Pottery tools can also be used to incise, with a more dramatic effect. Since they tend to take away a larger concentration of wax, oil paint can be less effective in coloring the incisions. By carefully applying colored wax to the area, then gently removing the excess with a scraping tool, a thick, colorful line is revealed.

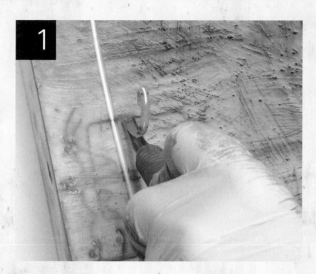

Carve deep lines in the wax
Use pottery carving tools to create deep lines in the wax.

Overfill area with wax
With warm wax in the color of your choice (I'm using Sap Green here), fill the area in and around the carved line. Overfilling—laying the paint on thickly—is necessary to give you a surface to carve back through.

Scrape cool wax away
Let the wax cool completely. With a razor blade or another scraping tool, gently remove the excess wax from the carved line. Use a gentle hand and scrape continuously until the line is revealed to your desired clarity.

A CLOSER LOOK

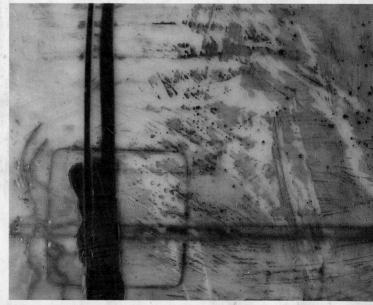

A closer look shows the full effect created by incisions in encaustic.

ABC'S

In this piece I used metal punch letter presses to create a fun compostition by randomly pressing the letters into the wax. I then rubbed varying concentrations of an oil paint stick over the impressions, completely coloring some while allowing the previous layers of encaustic paint to show through others.

GOLDEN

The oil paint and paint stick glazing on this incised piece emphasizes both the incised lines and the textural brushstrokes of the dry-brushed wax application.

ALIZARON

This piece was created by first incising heavy brushstrokes into layers of encaustic paint, then rubbing oil paint into the textured lines.

BORDER BRICK WALL

This piece was created as part of a series about the United States/Mexico border fence. The series features fences, walls and Southwestern icons to represent the two sides of the border. I used a book binder's needle tool to incise the bricks in this piece, then rubbed dark oil paint into the grooves.

MAKING IMPRESSIONS WITH A STENCIL

In addition to removing areas of wax for texture, you can also build layers up through the use of a metal stencil, which makes an impression in one layer of wax as you apply another to add further texture and interest. Stencils can be anything from products specifically designed for the purpose to interesting laces, screening or, as I've used here, punchella.

WHAT YOU'LL NEED

previously painted or primed board

encaustic paint in colors of your choosing

oil paint or paint stick in colors of your choosing

paintbrush

heat gun or other fusing tool

punchella or other metal stencil form

paper towel

rubber gloves

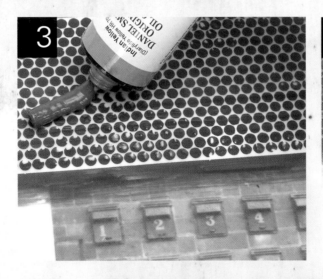

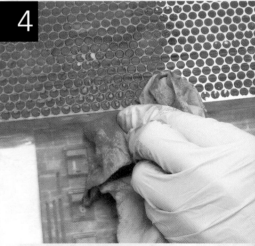

Paint over stencil

Choose something to serve as a stencil to add texture to your piece, and brush over it with a solid color of encaustic paint. Here, I've chosen a piece of punchella and a Burnt Umber encaustic medium.

Fuse and lift stencil

Give the wax a quick fuse with the ribbon still adhered in order to maintain the sharp edges the texture will offer. Then peel the punchella back while the wax is still warm to reveal the texture it created.

Apply coordinating color to textured area

Apply oil paint (straight from the tube, or from an oil paint stick) over the texture created by the punchella.

Rub in color and remove excess

Wearing rubber gloves to protect your hands, rub the color into the light areas of the board wherever you'd like. Remove the excess oil paint with a paper towel.

A CLOSER LOOK

A closer look at the finished piece created with the stencil on the opposite page shows the layers of color over the punchella's impressions.

1ST ENCOUNTER

I used punchella and drywall seam tape—as well as a great deal of textural brush work and square cookie cutters—to create a highly textured surface in this painting, which I then glazed with oil paint (see page 28). In addition, I added letter stickers (see page 40) to establish a focal point and add a bit of meaning to the piece.

SCRAPING

Scraping is simply the removal of built-up layers of wax. Using pottery scraping tools, putty knives or razor blades, you can use this technique to work through five to eight layers of wax (any fewer and it's not as interesting—any more and you'll tend not to get back to the original color), applying gentle strokes with the scraping tool until you achieve the desired visual effect. This technique can be meditative and relaxing. It can also create beautiful paintings and backgrounds for more work.

primed board

encaustic paints in 5-8 colors of your choosing

heat gun or other fusing tool

paintbrush

razor blade or other scraping tool

1

2

Layer color and fuse

Apply several layers of color, fusing between each one (here I layered a total of six colors). Vary the texture as you add the wax—that is, resist the urge to work it completely smooth; this will allow for more visual interest once you begin employing the scraping technique in the following steps. Once you're satisfied with the look you've created, let the board cool completely.

Scrape surface to reveal layers beneath

After the board has cooled completely, begin scraping off the top layer with a razor blade to start revealing the one underneath. Don't try to remove too much in one scrape. Take your time and try to apply a steady, even hand.

3

brush up

Put the painting in the refrigerator or freezer to speed the cooling process. I often work several pieces at once so that I can be working on one while the other cools.

Finish textured effect

Continue scraping, varying the direction of your blade and of your stroke, until portions of each color show through in an effect you like.

BACK FROM BLACK

This scraping painting was done a bit differently from the one shown on the opposite page. The wax was applied in layered circular patterns rather than flat surface layers. The removal process revealed these and gave the piece a more stylized, less abstract look.

SPRING

Here the wax layering was done by completely covering each subsequent layer. In scraping back, each layer of color was revealed sporadically, creating a purely abstract painting.

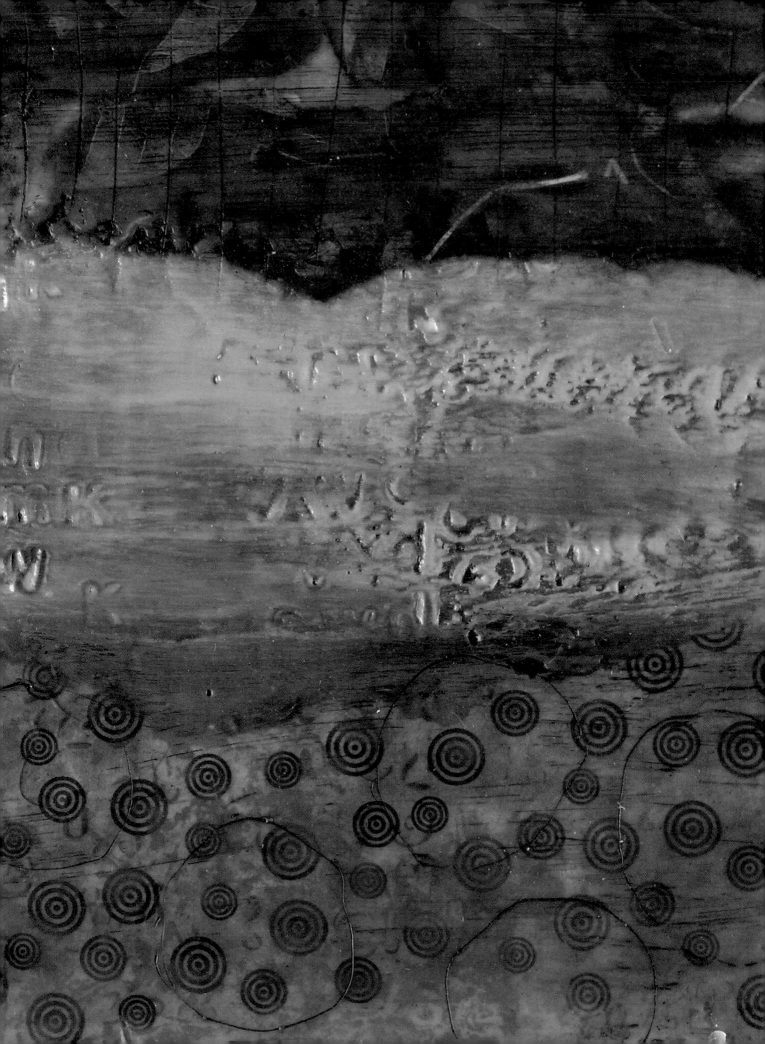

Lay IT ON

Collage in encaustic can open up your eyes to a whole new arena of possibilities. When layered with clear medium, richly colored, textured or patterned papers can take the place of pigmented wax in adding color and interesting depth to encaustic painting. Lightweight tissue papers become virtually translucent "drawn in" images; scraps of paper, strings and other found objects are rejuvenated with new life once embedded in the wax. In this chapter, we'll explore how easy it is to create layered and meaningful collages with encaustic as your glue.

"The prize is in the process."
Baron Baptiste

LIGHTWEIGHT PAPER AND STICKERS

When it comes to gathering supplies for this technique, I must confess I adore the scrapbooking department of the craft store. So many patterned papers—not to mention interesting stickers and doodads—have been created for scrapbooking that it's hard to resist using them in encaustic collage work. Explore your local aisles, and you'll get hooked by all the possibilities, too. You can create a wonderful encaustic collage by layering lightweight papers. They lie down nicely, even on top of one another, and often become transparent in the wax, offering an unexpected delight in the creation.

WHAT YOU'LL NEED

primed board

clear medium

heat gun or other fusing tool

paintbrush

lightweight paper(s) of your choosing

stickers

razor blade

1 Begin layering papers
Position your first layer of paper, apply a coat of medium, fuse, then move on to the next layer.

2 Continue to add layers
Continue building layers, applying a clear coat of medium and fusing after each one. Here I've added a vertical strip of paper and established a very satisfying combination of color.

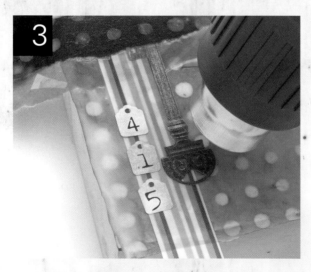

3 Add interest with stickers
Add stickers to create an interesting focal point in the wax. Simply place the stickers on the cooled wax surface and fuse them to the layers of paper and medium beneath. It is not necessary to apply a final layer of medium, but if you choose to, it will help reinforce the surface of your piece.

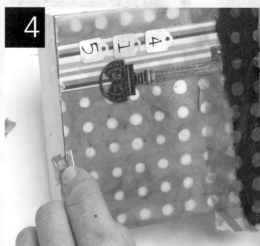

4 Clean up edges
Once the painting has cooled, use a razor blade to trim the excess paper from the edges.

A CLOSER LOOK

A closer look at the finished piece shows how lightweight papers and stickers can enhance an encaustic composition.

SUBURBAN SUN

In Suburban Sun, the color comes from lightweight papers in the wax. The composition was further enhanced by some techniques we'll learn on the following pages: the addition of found objects (see page 50) and rub-ons (see page 62).

TISSUE PAPER AND PASTELS

Using dry pastels, oil pastels or charcoal on Japanese silk tissue or another type of tissue paper is a great way to let your creativity shine and to incorporate interesting line work and drawings into your encaustic work. Again, the tissue virtually disappears in the wax, making it seem as if the drawing is part of the wax painting.

WHAT YOU'LL NEED

primed board

clear medium

heat gun or other fusing tool

paintbrush

silk tissue

dry pastel, several colors

1

Create design on paper
Draw the design or subject of your choice on the silk tissue with several layered colors of dry pastel.

2

Add paper to primed surface
On a warm, primed board, lay the tissue onto the wax and gently press to eliminate any air bubbles.

3

Brush on medium and fuse
Finish with another coat of clear medium. The pastel has a tendency to run a bit in the hot wax, so be mindful of your brushstrokes, depending on whether or not you like the blurred effect. (I like to brush my coat of clear medium in one direction only.) Re-fuse the layer.

brush up

In perfecting this technique, apply the wax in one direction with even, complete strokes to draw the pastel consistently through the painting. Here I worked from top to bottom to pull the wax through the pastel and down the board.

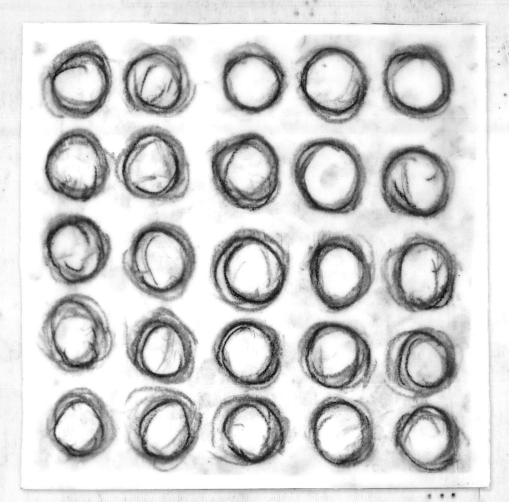

ALL

In this more elaborate piece, you can more clearly see how the "disappearing" tissue technique demonstrated on the opposite page makes it look as if the pastel drawing had been done directly in the wax.

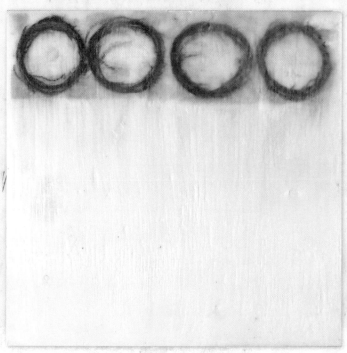

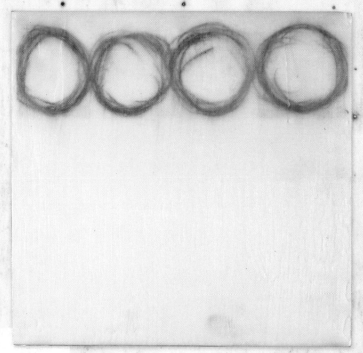

ORANGE *(at left);* BLUE *(at right)*

These pieces feature a variation of the technique shown on the opposite page. For this effect, rather than starting with tissue paper, simply coat the board's surface with a layer of medium and then, while it's still warm, "drag" the pastels through the surface. The hot wax pulls the pastel down into the layer as it's applied, resulting in a slightly less defined look.

LIGHTWEIGHT INK-JET PRINTS

I am an avid amateur photographer—aren't we all in this digital age?—so I was thrilled to find a way to incorporate ink-jet printed images in encaustic work. Japanese silk tissue paper and sumi paper work beautifully for creating a surface that will disappear into the wax and fluidly integrate the photo into the painting. To print photos on lightweight paper, simply cut the paper of your choice to 8½" × 11" (22cm × 28cm) and adhere it, with clear tape across the top edge, flush to a piece of text-weight paper before feeding it through the printer.

1

WHAT YOU'LL NEED

primed board ✳ *medium* ✳ *heat gun or other fusing tool*
paintbrush ✳ *printed piece of sumi or tissue paper*

Press image into warm, primed surface

Start with a primed board and, while it is still warm, press your piece of printed sumi or tissue paper into it, then apply additional medium over the top to seal it in. Fuse. (Turn to page 34 to see how this particular work became an underpainting for a more elaborate stenciled piece.)

FABRIC

Fabrics are fun to use for varied effects in encaustic collages. Having been sewing since an early age, and having a large collection of fabric on hand, I adore textiles as much as I do papers and have discovered this new use for them with great joy. Try this technique to incorporate a single fabric as a background for a section or the entire surface of your work, or combine different fabric scraps to make a sort of collage. You'll want to experiment with various thicknesses of medium to see how you can let the true textures and colors of the fabric show through and, conversely, how you can mask them in the depths of your wax.

1

WHAT YOU'LL NEED

primed board ✳ *medium* ✳ *heat gun or other fusing tool*
paintbrush ✳ *1 or more scraps of fabric*

Layer wax and add fabric

Prime your board with plenty of wax layers; I recommend laying the wax on thick up front to compensate for the absorbency of the fabric. Then, press the fabric gently into the warm wax surface to ensure there are no air bubbles. Brush medium over the fabric and fuse. It can often take several additional layers of medium to embed fabric thoroughly into the piece, especially with heavyweight fabrics that absorb a lot of wax.

TRIPLICATE

Combining contrasting weights of fabrics can make for a finished piece with a nice sense of depth. In this piece, the background fabric is a heavyweight burlap, the front is a lightweight silk and the final, almost invisible, fabric is a thin sheer weave. All three scraps were left behind from students of one of my workshops in Mendocino. Incorporating significant items into your work can commemorate a memory of where you've been.

HEAVYWEIGHT PAPER

I recommend moving on to this technique only after you've conquered the techniques for working with lightweight paper outlined on the previous pages. Heavyweights tend to have a mind of their own in the wax and will often want to lift out of the wax, resist lying flat and, quite frankly, drive you crazy. But once you're ready for a challenge, you can create some wonderful effects that are worth the hassle.

WHAT YOU'LL NEED

primed board

encaustic paints in color(s) of your choosing

medium

heat gun or other fusing tool

paintbrush

heavyweight paper

needle or other pointed metal tool

Create thick wax base

Apply several layers of a solid color of wax paint onto your surface to ensure a secure base for the paper to set into. Here I've painted layers of Sap Green. Then come back over with medium to prevent the color from bleeding into the paper when you lay it into the wax (unless, of course, that is the effect you want). Note: The medium will look milky while it is warm, but will become clearer as it cures and cools. Depending on how many layers have been applied, this can take as little as an hour to as much as several days.

Add heavyweight paper

While the wax is still warm, set the paper into the wax and press gently to ensure no air bubbles are trapped underneath. (Here I've used a piece of a water-color painting that was done on 140-lb. [300gsm] watercolor paper.) Apply another coat of medium over the paper.

brush up

If your heavyweight paper is not cooperating and is resisting your efforts to get it to lay flat on the surface, consider just letting the paper have its own way. The curling corners lend a spontaneous look to the finished piece.

Fuse while securing paper

Heavyweight paper has a tendency to curl at the edges and lift up off the wax. To make it lie flat, fuse the surface again while using a pointer tool to hold the corner down gently as you work. Be careful: Using a lot of force will only damage the wax underneath.

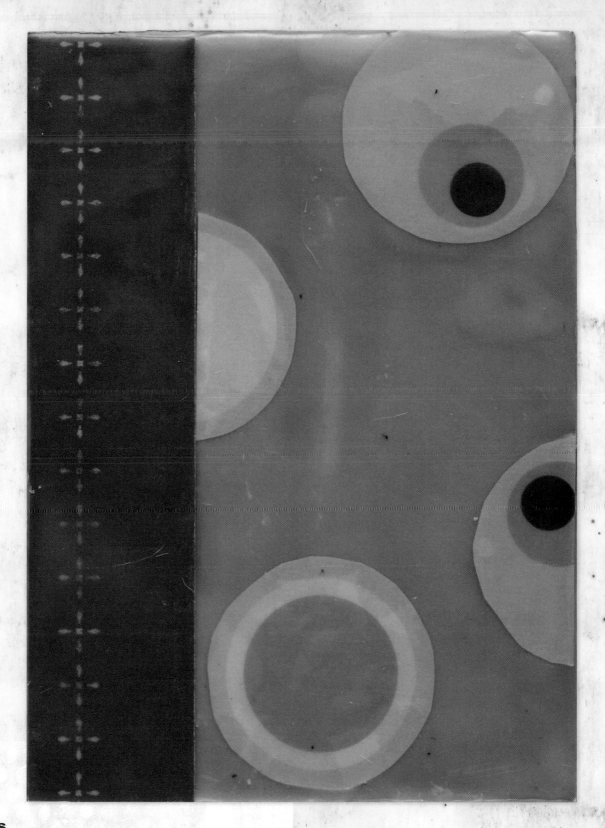

MEASLES

This painting combines several heavyweight papers in the wax, including circles cut from a patterned paper and a favorite red scrap from my collection. Here you can see that with a little finessing, all the papers behaved and laid down flat in the wax.

METALLIC LEAF

I have a confession: I had never experimented with metallic leaf before deciding to try it in my encaustic work, so I can't make any firsthand comparisons between incorporating this fun substance into wax and other mediums. But I can tell you that I loved the results. You can leave the finish shiny or coat it with thick layers of medium for a more subdued look.

primed board

heat gun or other fusing tool

sheet of metallic leaf

medium (optional)

paintbrush (optional)

Press primed board onto leaf

Open a sheet of metallic leaf from its original packaging and lay it facedown on your surface. (There is no need to remove it from its backing or to add any of the traditional leaf adhesive.) Place a warm, primed board facedown onto the leaf, and press firmly on the board. The warm wax will grab the leaf and create a gentle adhesion.

Fuse slowly

Using a low air flow setting, fuse the leaf to the primed layer.

brush up

If you opt to brush medium over the top of the leaf, let the medium cool, then buff it up to bring back some of the shine.

Coat with additional wax (optional)

The leafing can then be covered with more hot wax, or simply left as the shiny final layer. Here I've added wax to half of the finished surface so you can see both end results. As you can see, the luminosity of the metal leaf is lost under the wax, but it still lends an interesting element to the painting. If you choose to leave the leaf exposed, keep in mind that it will be fragile and susceptible to scratches.

RED METAL

This painting began with a variegated red metallic leaf. Even with layers of beeswax over it, the variegated tones show through, and the metallic still shimmers a bit. I love the visual texture you can achieve with this technique.

FOUND OBJECTS

Dimensional elements can be really fun to incorporate into wax. Experiment with adding any odds and ends you'd like to feature in your artwork. This technique lends itself to being combined with others to create a multi-layered work. Here I began with the piece I created using tissue paper and pastels on page 42. Then, to add interest and depth, I included some objects I discovered while walking in my neighborhood. You might also consider incorporating store-bought items, such as embellishments found in the scrapbooking aisles of your local craft store.

(page 42)

WHAT YOU'LL NEED

primed or previously painted board

medium

heat gun or other fusing tool

paintbrush

found objects of your choosing

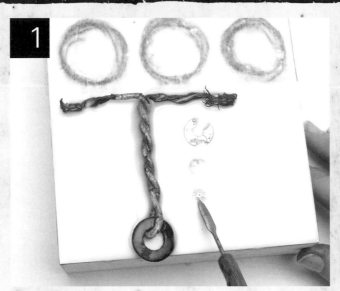

1

Build up thick layer of wax and press in objects

Start with a primed board and add medium to the depth you desire for your objects. Embedding objects can require extra wax for adhesion depending on the size and weight of the object. Fuse between layers. Once this foundation has been established, press the objects into the warm wax.

2

Embed items in wax

Brush additional medium over and around the objects to help hold them in place. Some objects may be thin enough to simply coat once, but others, like this one, require several applications.

brush up

If you are trying to paint over elements and they're moving around too much, try drizzling the medium over them instead, then overfusing. This should keep them in place and allow you to achieve a thick but smooth surface.

PERFECT FIT

Using the work I created on the opposite page as inspiration, I created this larger composition by using a similar found object, adding key and lock stickers (see page 40), incising (see page 28), subtly transferring an image (see page 58) and adding texture by drybrushing. All of this was done with natural, unrefined beeswax—rather than the clear, refined wax—in order to utilize its natural yellow coloring.

FIBERS

Textile elements of all kinds lend themselves to inclusion in your encaustic works—and that means more than just fabric. String, yarn, ribbons and raffia can all create interesting layers in your wax. I find this technique wonderful for showing the unique depth of encaustic; where the threads overlap, you can see one literally suspended in wax above the other.

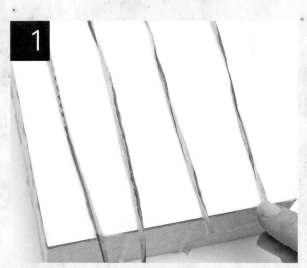

Lay first layer into warm, primed board.

Start with a warm primed board and press the fibers of your choice into it just as you'd do with paper or fabric. Here my goal is to create a grid pattern of strings that will showcase the visual depth achievable in hot wax, so I'm starting with the bottom layer only.

Coat first layer with medium

Brush a layer of medium over the strands. Fuse the surface.

Press second layer into warm wax

Add another layer of strings (here I'm working in the opposite direction to showcase the depth of the work). Brush on additional medium, and fuse again.

Continue to layer string with medium

Continue in this manner, adding layers of string and medium, until you've created the depth you want in the layers. Once the final coat of medium has been applied and fused, trim the excess string from the edges with scissors or a razor blade.

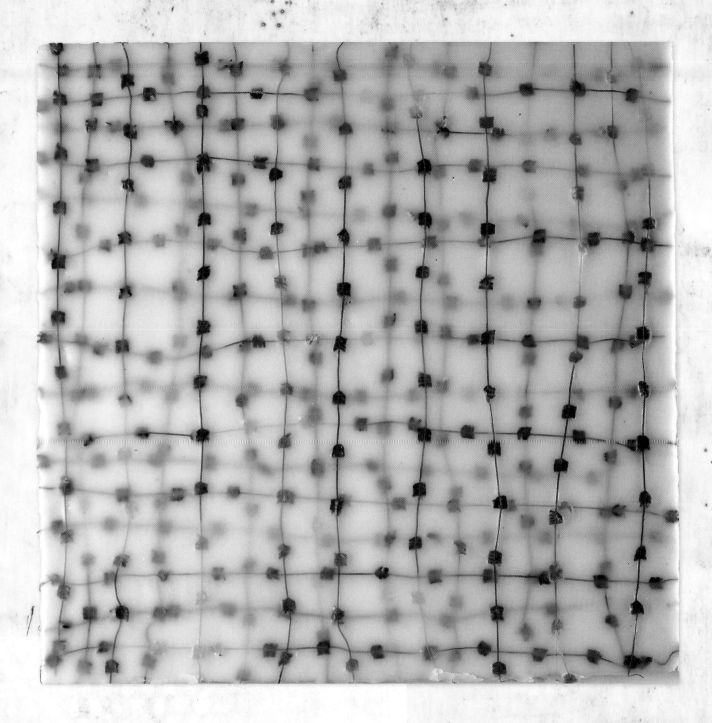

COLOR SQUARE

You can create even more depth by layering a more dimensional fiber—like this rainbow-colored string yarn with fiber "flags"— in between layers of clear medium.

NATURAL ELEMENTS

Adding natural elements to your encaustic works is one of the purest ways to enhance the organic look and feel of the beeswax medium. Literally anything you can encase in wax can be added to an encaustic painting, so keep your eyes peeled for interesting leaves, stones, shells and feathers to include in your work. You never know what interesting effects you can create until you try. Here I've used some shells, small stones, sand and a leaf skeleton.

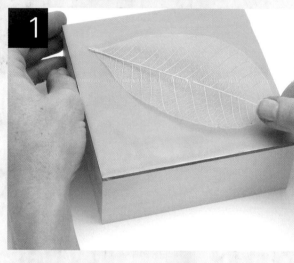

Press object into warm wax
Start with a warm, primed or re-fused encaustic surface and gently lay your first natural element into position. Here I've started with a coat of King's Blue wax paint and set a leaf skeleton gently into the surface.

Coat and fuse
Brush a layer of clear medium over the top of the object and re-fuse.

Add additional elements
Add texture and increase the organic appearance of your piece by sprinkling elements such as dirt, ash, sand or soot into the second coat of warm wax and re-fusing. When re-fusing elements like sand, keep the heat gun at a distance from the surface (and on a low speed, if possible) to avoid blowing it all away; the wax should still warm enough to absorb and adhere the sand.

Add largest items last
Finally, add larger, more dimensional elements as your final layer, with coats of additional medium brushed around them to hold them in place.

A closer look at the completed piece shows the lovely organic texture and composition that can be created by adding natural elements to encaustic art.

SITKA

This piece was created with objects collected on a trip to the Oregon coast. The sizes and textures of the sticks and pinecones fit in nicely with the yellow tone of the natural, unrefined beeswax.

KISS

kiss

KISS \KIS\ v. 1. TO TOUCH SOMEBODY OR SOMETHING WITH THE LIPS 2. TO TOUCH OR BRUSH AGAINST SOMETHING LIGHTLY

IMPORTANT FOLLOW THESE EASY DIRECTIONS STEP BY STEP

Rub
IT IN

If you're like most mixed-media artists and crafters, at some point you probably have tried your hand at one or more image-transfer techniques. Polaroid, gel medium, chemical: There are many different methods, and you probably already know that they're not all consistently successful or mess free. So I invite you to join the encaustic image transfer revolution. You'll find the techniques in this chapter so easy, so satisfying and so beautiful that soon your imagination will be overflowing with ideas for your own work.

We'll start by learning a traditional image transfer. If you're an avid photographer like me, chances are you'll enjoy transferring your own original photos to your encaustic work as much as I do—but you can also experiment with clip art, words and numbers, maps, blueprints and even graphic designs. We'll then move on to see how rub-ons, charcoal rubbings, graphite paper and even metallic leaf can be used to transfer simple images, characters or accents to your work.

> "It is not what you see that is the art: Art is the gap."
> **Marcel Duchamp**

IMAGE TRANSFERS

To get the best image transfer using this technique, I recommend using a fresh photocopy of an ink-jet printed image, but laser-printer images also work. Be mindful that the image needs to be carbon- or toner-based rather than ink-based; otherwise, the ink will just smear on the wax rather than transferring clearly. I love the effects created by transferring black-and-white images with this method, but it also works well with color images. Experiment with both and see what you like best.

Trim image and place facedown in warm wax

Trim the photocopied image to the desired size. Begin with a warm, primed surface and lay your image facedown into the wax.

Saturate paper with water

Pour enough water on the back of the paper to saturate it. The water is needed to remove the paper from the transferred image itself.

Burnish thoroughly

Burnish the image. I like to use the back of a metal spoon because of the concave shape and, of course, because metal tools make for easy use and easy cleanup. Be sure to burnish the entire image, as any missed areas will not transfer. There's no need to be gentle; if the wax is at the right temperature, you will not damage the surface. A firm hand is needed to ensure a good carbon transfer.

Burnish wet paper and remove pulp

Let the water sit on the paper for a minute or so to allow the paper to absorb it, then burnish again with the spoon. This will begin to "pulp" the paper and reveal the image set in the wax. Once this happens, begin rubbing the paper off with your fingers.

5

Fuse transferred image

Once you are satisfied that the paper has been removed, fuse the transfer. The heat will warm the wax and cause any small paper fibers to become absorbed and disappear.

Transferring a color image

Use the same technique for color transfer. To best illustrate the different effects, I've used different versions of the same image—a close-up of some interesting mushrooms I found in my front yard—in both transfers.

LIVING BACKWARDS

Image transfers can be used to add meaning to a work. Here I've intentionally placed the transfer in reverse to exemplify the place I was at in my life during this painting period.

MY NEIGHBOR'S FORT

This piece began with a landscape blueprint transfer with interesting line work and loosely defined images. It allowed me to maintain my abstract, emotional painting while developing an interesting focal point.

13

This piece is a result of experimentation with image transferring, layering and depth. The landscape design was done in the first layer of encaustic, followed by several layers of medium, then the image transfer was added. The result shows depth while maintaining clear imagery at each layer.

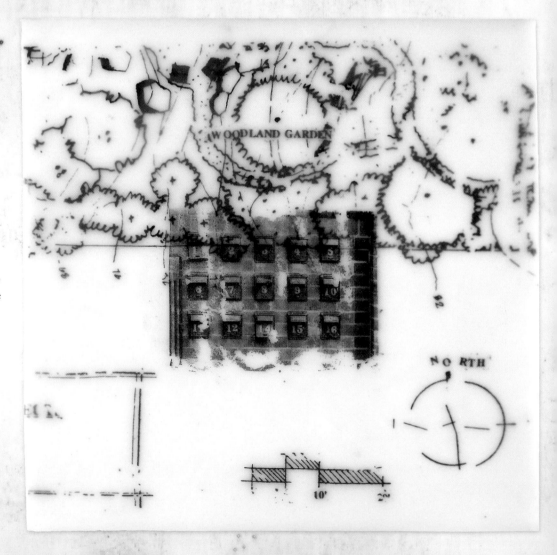

SANTA FE

This piece features a color transfer of a photograph I took in Santa Fe. The top is textured with a stencil (see page 34). The flecks of color come from bits of wax that were embedded in the stencil and melted into the wax as I painted over the stencil. I really like the unintentional effect!

INTUITION

The simple inclusion of an image transfer in this encaustic collage serves as a gentle focal point for the bright, strong colors of the patterned papers that add a great deal of punch.

RUB-ONS

Rub-ons are another of my favorite finds from the scrapbooking aisles of my local craft store. Transferring these oh-so-cool ready-made elements—featuring words, numbers, scrolls and pretty much anything else you can imagine—is as simple as removing the backing and burnishing the image with the tool provided. The result is an amazingly clean and seamless look.

WHAT YOU'LL NEED

primed or previously painted board with a cool wax surface ✳ *heat gun or other fusing tool* *rub-on embellishment* ✳ *craft stick or other burnishing tool*

Apply rub-on and re-fuse
Rub on lettering or imagery can be burnished onto a cool board quite simply by using the craft stick that is included in the package. Fuse your surface once the rub-on is completely transferred. Here I'm rubbing some text onto the image-transfer piece I created on page 58.

METALLIC LEAF TRANSFERS

Oh, the joy of a pop of metallic glitz! Even if a shiny finish isn't normally your style, you may be surprised to find that just a touch of some cleverly applied gold or silver leaf can add that oh-so-perfect final touch to your encaustic works. Rather than imbedding the leaf (as we learned on page 48), this time we'll be rubbing it onto the surface for an entirely different effect.

WHAT YOU'LL NEED

primed or previously painted board with a cool wax surface ✳ *heat gun or other fusing tool* *metallic leaf* ✳ *scribing tool or ball-end stylus*

Impress leaf into wax
Lay the leaf onto a cool wax surface. Use a scribing tool or a ball-end stylus to impress the foil into the wax in the desired areas.

Reveal transfer and fuse
Peel up the leaf to reveal the transfer. Fuse this section of the surface if you are satisfied or, as with any added element, if you don't like the end result, simply scrape it off and begin again.

022007

For this black-and-white composition, I began with multiple photo transfers: first the landscape design, then the numbers from a collage paper that I had scanned, then printed as a toner-based copy. The subtle rub-on transfer of the word "boy" added depth. Finally, I incised the surface with a bit of textural brushwork, then glazed the surface with black oil paint to emphasize the texture (see page 28).

ROUGHING IT

Sometimes happy accidents can make for unexpected works of art. By simply laying the metallic leaf over the rough, textural surface I'd created in this piece, then burnishing the whole area, I created these sporadic metallic touches. The effect wasn't what I was initially trying to achieve, but I came to love the look and decided it was a finished piece.

CARBON AND GRAPHITE PAPER

Art supply stores carry graphite and carbon papers in their drawing supply areas. Pick up a box—they come in colors!—and start experimenting with this fun and simple transfer technique.

WHAT YOU'LL NEED

primed or previously painted board with a cool wax surface ✳ *carbon or graphite paper* *stylus or other scribing tool*

Transfer as you would metallic leaf

Carbon (shown here) or graphite paper can be used to quickly and easily transfer sketches or writing onto a board. Simply use the same technique for application described for metallic leaf on page 62. Here I'm using this technique to add further detail to the image-transfer piece I created on page 58.

GRAPHITE AND CHARCOAL RUBBINGS

Using vellum and a graphite or charcoal stick, you can create abstract rubbings of virtually any surface you like, and then transfer them to encaustic works for a look that is both distressed and dimensional. Do you remember doing grave-marker rubbings in elementary school? They're back!

WHAT YOU'LL NEED

primed or painted board with a cool wax surface ✳ *heat gun or other fusing tool* ✳ *vellum* *charcoal or graphite* ✳ *burnishing tool*

Burnish rubbing onto cool wax surface

Create a rubbing or drawing on vellum with charcoal or graphite. Pictured is a charcoal rubbing of the texture of an adobe wall in Sante Fe. Set the vellum facedown on a cool, primed or painted board. Burnish with the back of a spoon or a similar burnishing tool.

Reveal transfer and fuse

Peel off the paper to reveal the transfer. If you're not happy with the resulting effect, simply place the vellum back on your surface and continue rubbing. When you've created a look you like, re-fuse.

MUCH LOVE

In this piece, I used a ball-tip stylus to journal some stream of consciousness thoughts on a sheet of graphite transfer paper placed directly on the painted wax. I then overfused the words with a heat gun, causing some of the graphite to disperse and make the enclosed message more subtle and partially hidden.

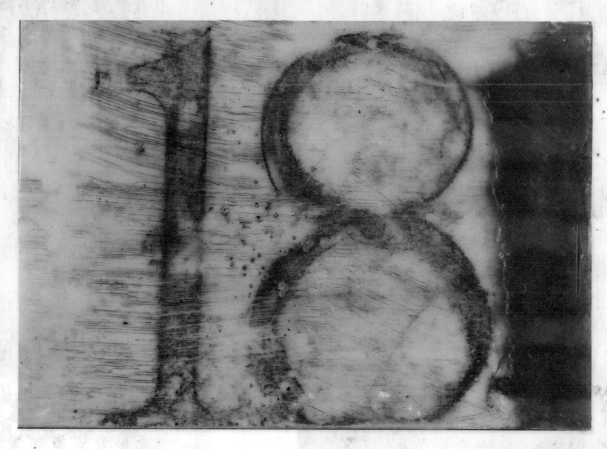

HOME

Here I applied the charcoal rubbing of the number 18 directly to the cooled, primed surface. I then added the collage element of the medium-weight colored paper, then used Quinacridone Rose oil paint to glaze the entire surface and to fill the incised brush strokes with additional color (see page 28).

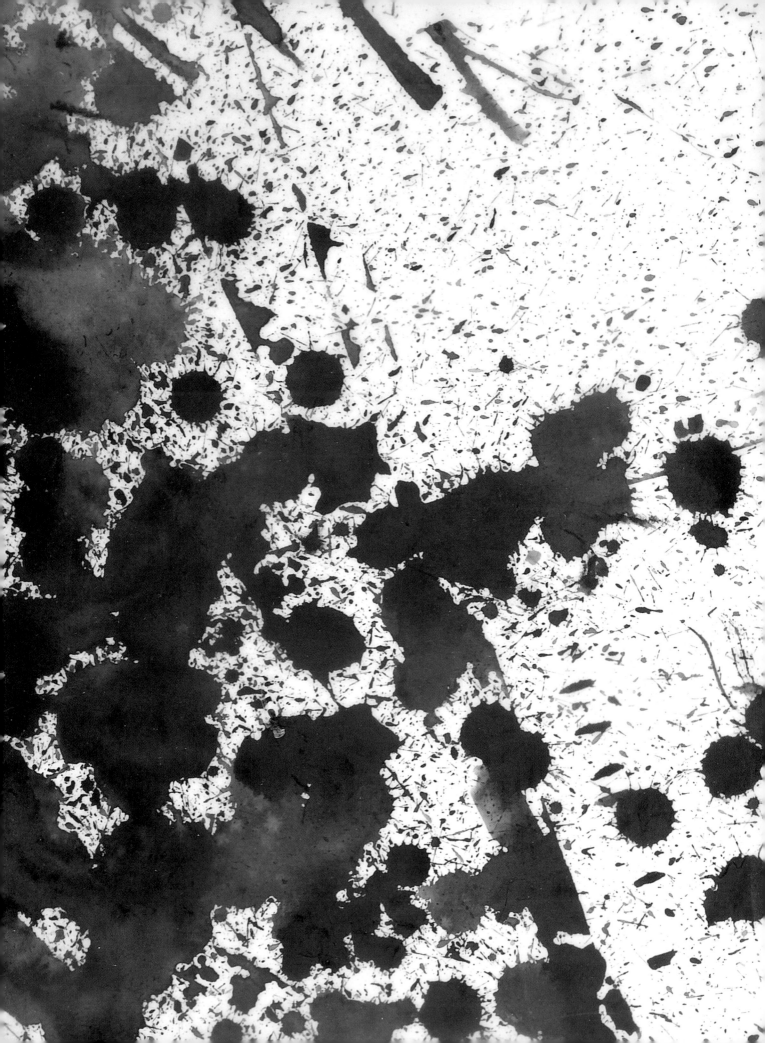

Break
THE RULES

Admit it: You experiment with your art. Otherwise, you wouldn't be interested in this book. Now that you've learned some of my most tried-and-true encaustic techniques, it's time to join me as we test the boundaries, push the limits, explore every "What if?" and play, incorporating everything from watercolor paint to shellac in encaustic experiments. That is where invention begins. Any artist who works from the creative side that says "Why not?" and "Who says I can't try it?" has dipped a toe into the experimentation that leads to creative invention and surprises of unpredictable beauty. It has been enlivening to explore the boundless possibilities in encaustic. But I'm sure I haven't broken all the rules myself—yet. Don't limit yourself to the ideas you find in this chapter, what you learn in a workshop or what other artists tell you: Explore and push the envelope of your own creativity. You may be pleasantly surprised with the results.

"There is no must in art because art is free."

Wassily Kandinsky

CHARCOAL

Who says you can't combine mediums in encaustic? Drawing with charcoals, pastels or graphite onto your surface before you've even primed the board is a lot of fun. I have always enjoyed doodling (thanks, Mom and Dad!) and tend to come away from a meeting or conference with scribbles and marks down the margins of all my note pages. If you're a doodler like me, or if you enjoy sketching, you'll love this technique.

1

Draw on unprimed surface
Draw directly onto an unprimed board with charcoal, pastel or graphite. I tend to favor free-flowing, organic lines like those shown here.

2

Heat surface and add medium
Heat the board as if to prime it, and apply a coat of medium. The charcoal, graphite or pastel may smear a bit, but this can have wonderful effects—use it to your advantage! Fuse to finish, or add additional layers of medium, transparent colors or other elements, treating this as an underpainting for a more in-depth work.

WHAT YOU'LL NEED

unprimed board

medium

heat gun or other fusing tool

paintbrush

charcoal, pastel or graphite

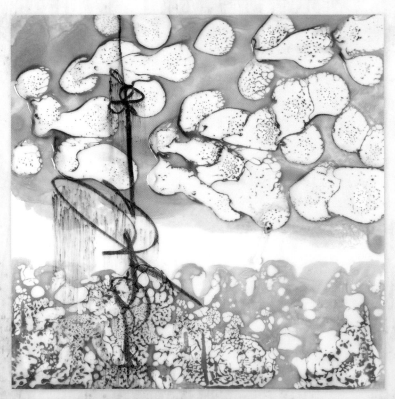

Turn to page 76 to see how this charcoal work became an underpainting for a piece using the dry shellac technique.

BLOBS

For this piece, rather than sketching right on the unprimed board, I doodled with charcoal on watercolor paper, then adhered it to the board and applied a coat of encaustic medium to create this effect.

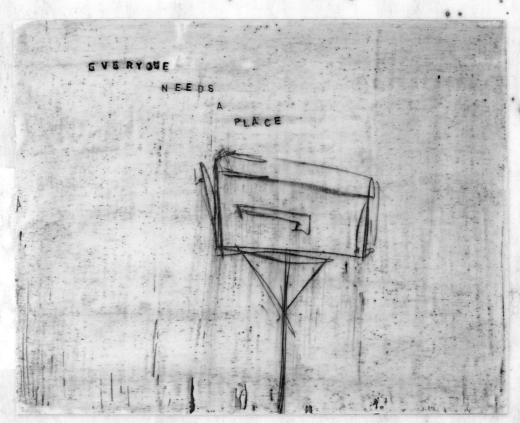

EVERYONE NEEDS A PLACE

A graphite pencil drawing directly on the board created the focal point for this gentle piece. Metal letter stamps pressed into a top layer of medium pair with brushstroke incising and black oil paint glazing (see page 28) to complete the effect.

STAMPS

I had never used stamping in my work until I decided one day that I wanted to use some abstract stamped images as an underpainting. I asked some scrapbooking wizards which ink to use; they recommended a pigment dye ink, and that's what I've gone with ever since. If you are familiar with stamping and all the options available, or if you carve your own stamps, use this technique to incorporate those images to create interesting base layers in your encaustic painting.

WHAT YOU'LL NEED

unprimed board

clear or tinted medium

heat gun or
other fusing tool

paintbrush

rubber stamp

ink

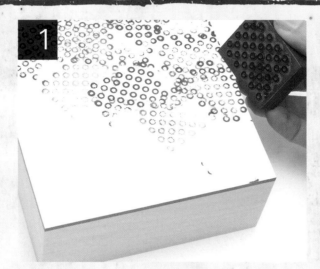

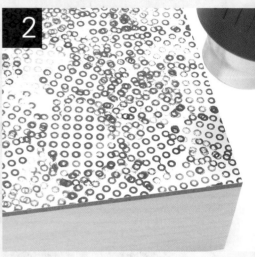

Stamp unprimed surface
Stamp directly onto an unprimed board with a rubber stamp and pigment ink. (The ink will not work well on a primed, waxed surface.)

Heat surface
Heat the surface, heat-setting the ink and warming the board for priming all at once.

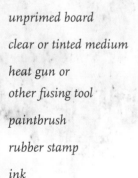

Brush on medium and fuse
Apply a layer of clear or tinted medium and fuse. Here I've opted for a transparent Quinacridone Magenta to exhibit how the stamped underpainting can show through and create a more subtle layered effect.

HIGH

This painting was created with the intent of using color and still maintaining the underpainting of stamped flowers. By diluting the color with clear beeswax to a mix of one part color to six parts beeswax, I was able to layer two applications of wax over the stamped Claybord without loosing the imagery. I love the way the image becomes distorted yet remains visible.

ALCOHOL INKS

Varied interesting effects can be created by adding alcohol inks to encaustic work.
The alcohol dries so quickly that it lends itself to a few different techniques.

GLAZING

1

On a primed board, alcohol ink allows you to create
a gentle, transparent glazing of color in the wax.

WHAT YOU'LL NEED

primed board ✻ *alcohol ink* ✻ *paper towel*

Add transparent color to primed surface

To create a transparent glaze of color on a
primed surface, first squeeze some alcohol ink
onto a paper towel, then rub it over the medium.
This method allows you to really rub the color
into the wax, creating a beautiful transparency.
(An added bonus is that you aren't left with
caked bristles or other tools to clean!) If you have
created texture in the wax before adding the ink,
the textured areas will pick up the ink more than
the smooth areas do, offering a variance of color.

UNDERPAINTING

1

On an unprimed board, you can use alcohol ink to
quickly set an underpainting into your surface.

Heat surface and apply medium

When the ink is dry, heat the board to set
the ink and simultaneously prepare the
board for priming. Apply a layer of clear or
tinted medium to create the desired effect.
Fuse to complete the work, or move on to
add additional layers.

WHAT YOU'LL NEED

unprimed board ✻ *medium* ✻ *heat gun or other fusing tool*
paintbrush ✻ *alcohol ink*

Apply ink to unprimed board

Apply ink to an unprimed board in any way you'd
like. You can paint it on with a brush, or apply it
directly from a bottle with an applicator tip.

2

A CLOSER LOOK

A closer look shows the wonderfully freeform effects created by applying alcohol ink straight from the bottles.

DOTS AND DASHES

This experimental piece resulted from simply playing with the ink on the board. I used a dropper and left each drop of ink thickly applied. Then, to finish the piece, I incised some detail lines into the piece (see page 28) and glazed the surface with a contrasting color of alcohol ink. The addition of a few collage elements balanced the composition.

WATERCOLOR

I am a watercolor junkie! I really enjoy fluid watercolors and try to use them in any application I can. Here is a great way to incorporate more than one medium into encaustic work with vibrant results.

Pool water on unprimed board

Start by pooling some water directly onto an unprimed board.

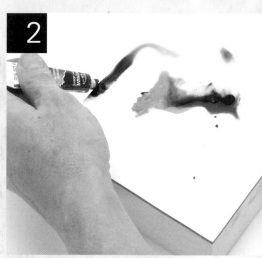

Apply watercolor directly from tube

Squeeze some small dollops of watercolor directly from the tube into the pool of water on the board. Add as many colors as you'd like; I've added 3.

Blend and spread paints

Use a brush to spread the color around and blend it together and with the water, as you choose. Or, you can also simply tilt the board to make the colors run and create some different effects, as I'm doing here.

Let dry, apply medium and fuse

When the watercolor is dry, apply a layer of medium over the board and then fuse it. This can be a finished work, or an underpainting for more layers of encaustic.

DOAK

In brushing encaustic over a watercolor painting, as I did here, the watercolors become richer and transform into a wonderful foundation for further techniques, or a luminous glazed painting in and of itself.

SPLATTERED

By dropping watercolor into puddles of water on the clean, unprimed board, I achieved color in this piece through watercolor abstraction before coating it with medium to heighten the colors and serve as a varnish.

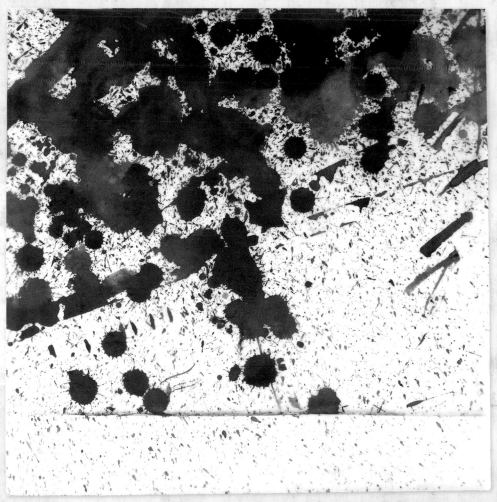

SHELLAC

Shellac may seem like an odd component to add to encaustic. After all, no sealant or finish is necessary in the encaustic medium, and shellac is stinky, caustic and messy. But by using these three variations on the shellac technique (all of which use the materials listed on the opposite page), you can combine the mediums while keeping the organic nature of encaustic.

DRY

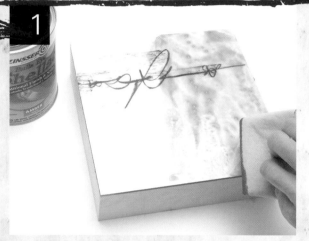

Dab shellac onto fused surface

Using a paper towel, dab shellac over a desired area or, if you prefer, over the entire primed board. (Here I am working over the piece I began with a charcoal scribble [see page 68]; it has been covered with a layer of medium and fused.) Allow the shellac layer to dry.

Of all the methods for adding shellac to encaustic, this one offers the most control in the process.

Burn holes into shellac

Use a butane torch to burn holes into the shellac layer. Begin by moving the torch directly into the shellac at a gentle rate until it begins to form one of the organic circles shown here. Pull the flame away once the circle is the size you desire. Continue in this way until you've worked the board to the desired effect.

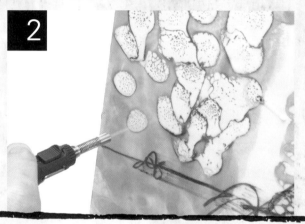

WET

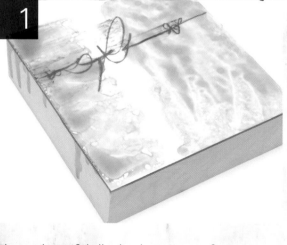

Apply and ignite shellac

Use a paper towel to dab the shellac on the primed board. Immediately light a match or use the torch to ignite the wet shellac.

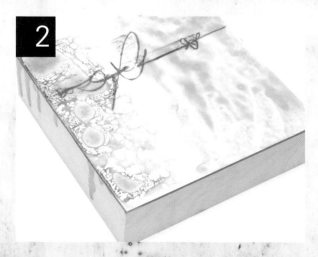

The wet burn of shellac has become one of my all-time favorite techniques—it's spontaneous and unpredictable.

Let it burn

Let the shellac burn until it burns itself out or, if you prefer, blow it out as soon as you like the effect.

WHAT YOU'LL NEED

*primed board * medium * paintbrush * shellac * mica powder (optional) * butane torch * matches * paper towel*

1

Apply medium

Apply a layer of medium over the surface. This is especially important if you're starting with a painted board, because it creates a barrier between the pigmented encaustic and the mica; otherwise, the color picks up the mica and dilutes its luminosity.

2

Add shellac and mica powder

Use a paper towel to dab shellac over the surface of the board. Sprinkle mica powder into the wet shellac.

3

Blend the powder and shellac

Use a paper towel to blend the mica powder into the shellac. (True to its unpredictable nature, sometimes the shellac picks up the mica powder on its own, in which case, you can skip this step.)

4

Burn shellac

Ignite the shellac with a match or the torch flame. Allow the shellac to burn out on its own, or blow it out yourself once you've achieved results you like.

brush up

When working with shellac, be cautious. If you are wary of open flames or potentially toxic fumes, this may not be the technique for you. To limit your contact with toxic substances, use paper towels for shellac application so you don't have to clean a brush with solvent with each use. Just be sure to dispose of the dirty towel properly, as shellac is flammable.

A CLOSER LOOK

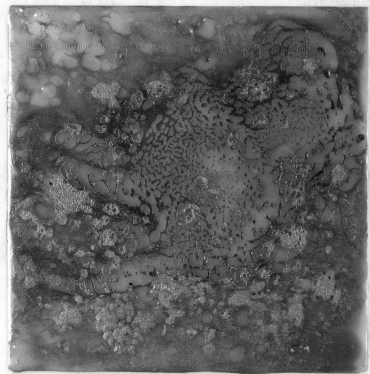

A closer look shows the sparkle mica powder adds to the wet shellac technique.

FIRE

A wet shellac burn was used in this aptly titled example. The beautiful, unpredictable nature of the wet burn leads to very organic, loose imagery.

ICE

This second example of the same technique shows that no two wet shellac burns are alike.

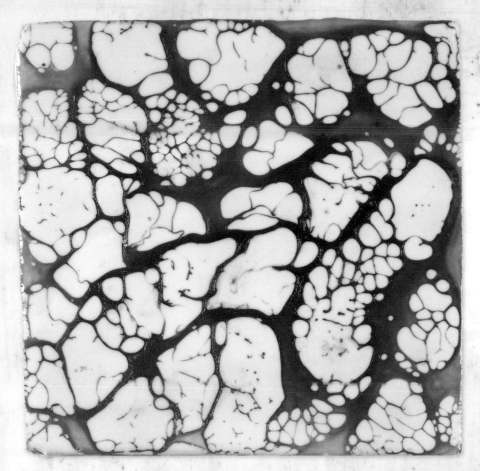

SNAIL TRAIL

In this dry shellac burn, more control and predictability are exemplified through this specific spot-burn technique.

CIRCLE ROUND

In Circle Round, the dry shellac burn technique is used in combination with incising and oil paint glazing (see page 28) as well as scraping (see page 36) to create a unified piece.

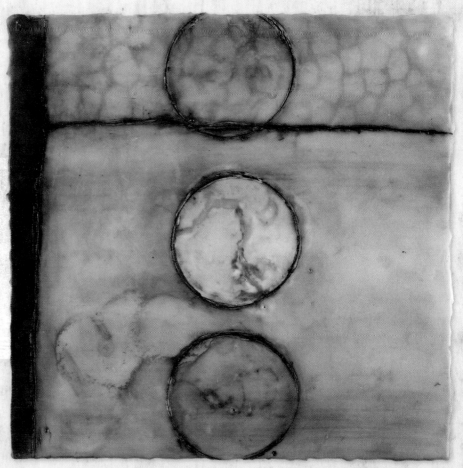

WHITE GLUE AND INSTANT TEA

I love any technique that creates new uses for things you probably already have around the house. You'll be amazed at what you can do with just some glue and instant tea!

WHAT YOU'LL NEED

unprimed board

medium or

natural beeswax

paintbrush

heat gun or other fusing tool

instant tea, unsweetened

white glue

Apply glue
On an unprimed board, squeeze out a puddle of white glue.

Sprinkle tea into wet glue
While the glue is still wet, sprinkle instant, unsweetened tea into it.

Heat to create texture
Heat the concoction with a heat gun until it begins to bubble. Continue heating until you've created the amount of texture you desire. It will begin to dry and burn in interesting patterns that can lend an intriguing start to your encaustic painting.

Prime surface
When the glue has dried completely, prime the board with a layer of medium. For an alternate look, I've found that using natural beeswax for priming the surface created by this technique yields a beautiful finished product.

brush up

Try using wood glue for this technique for a different effect; its yellow tint can achieve a more organic look.

A CLOSER LOOK

A closer look shows the interesting textures created by tea in the wax.

TEA FOR TWO

In this piece I applied the glue in a deliberate two-part division. I then sprinkled the tea over these two separate areas and burned just the larger area. I like how the two areas differ yet are of the same technique. The letters are stickers I simply positioned on the surface, then covered with medium, letting the edges peek through.

GOUACHE

Gouache and tempera applied over a primed board can offer an interesting, albeit unusual, look in the encaustic. In the heating process over the initial layers of wax, the gouache breaks up and creates interesting crack lines and fissures. These can be put to use as organic, visual texture layers as more medium is applied.

WHAT YOU'LL NEED

primed, painted or underpainted board

heat gun or other fusing tool

gouache

paper towels

paintbrush (optional)

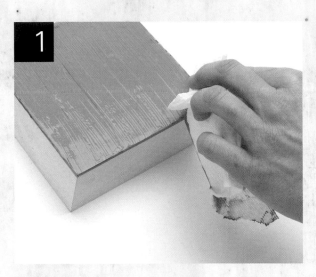

Squeeze gouache onto surface
Apply gouache directly from the tube onto a primed, painted or underpainted board of your choice. Spread it with paper towel or a brush to cover the surface.

Heat surface
Dry the paint on the wax with a heat gun. Continue in this manner until cracks develop. Play with the heat reaction until you are satisfied with the results.

A CLOSER LOOK

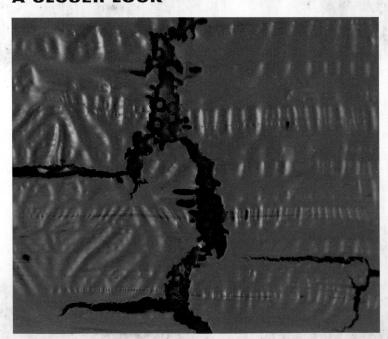

A closer look at the complete effect shows the opacity and texture of the gouache on the stamped background that was created on page 70.

CITY FOLK

The color in this piece comes from experimenting with a combination of wax, gouache layering and oil paint. The transfer of the landscape design (see page 58) adds a focal point, while figures sketched on Japanese tissue paper (see page 42) lend meaning to the piece. The loose movement of the colors happened as I was working over the warm surface and keeping my brush moving in the warm layers, rather than letting each layer dry to suspend it from the others.

BLEACHED PAPER

The effects created by bleach on black paper are gorgeous; there's no other way of putting it. I currently favor circles, as you can see in this example, but any design can be created with the cooler-than-cool bleach pens you can find in the laundry aisle of the grocery store.

WHAT YOU'LL NEED

unprimed board

medium

heat gun or
other fusing tool

paintbrush

black paper or
cardstock

bleach pen

clear medium or gel
medium (depending
on the paper's weight)

paper towels

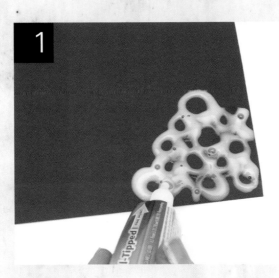

Draw design with bleach pen
On a piece of black paper or cardstock, create a design with a bleach pen.

Let it dry and brush off surface
Let the piece dry completely. Then, brush the dried bleach bits off of the surface with a paper towel.

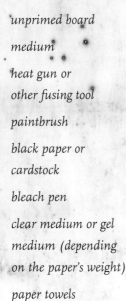

Apply medium
If your paper is thin, like rice paper, adhere it to your board with clear medium. If it's heavier, glue it to your surface with gel medium, let it dry, then apply a layer of medium and fuse.

brush up

The result of this technique is not a lightfast creation, even with the encaustic top layer, so keep in mind that some change to the color and intensity will occur over time.

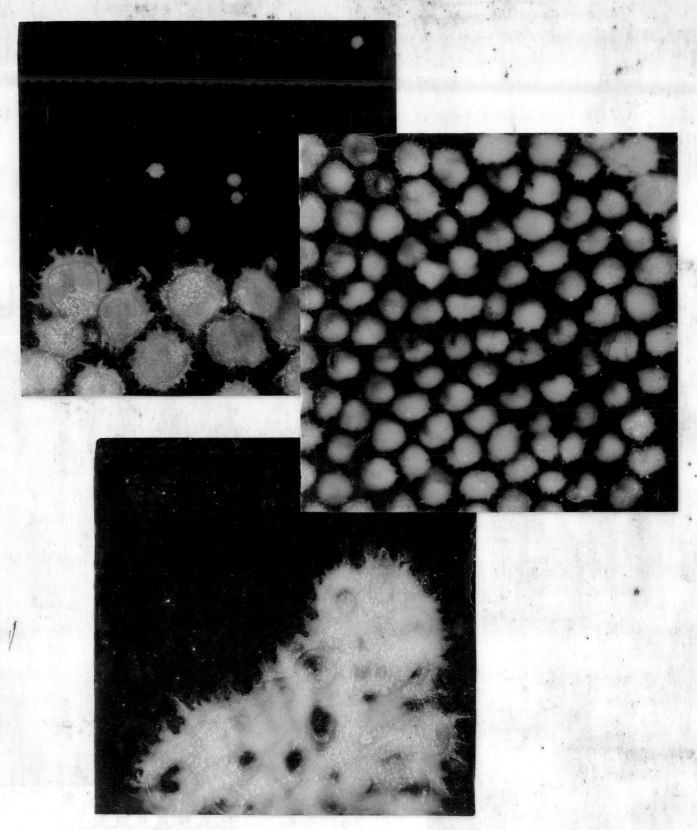

BLEACH TRIPTYCH

I created this triptych, a piece of three separate works intended to be displayed as one, on 5" × 5" (13cm × 13cm) Claybords. The use of the bleach paper technique made them very ethereal and resulted in pieces that can be effectively arranged in any number of combinations for a varied display.

Show IT OFF

Deep wooden boards like the Claybords shown throughout this book are ideal for simply wiring and hanging without frames. They lend a contemporary look to the painting that enhances the effect of the encaustic medium. I always use Claybords with a 2" (5cm) cradle (meaning the sides are 2" [5cm] deep and the back is hollowed out) for this reason. Not only does it make the Claybord a cost-effective option, it is gorgeous! If you prefer the ¾" (2cm) cradle, you can simply wire and hang it, as well, though the option to frame it in a canvas floater frame is also available.

The first step in readying a Claybord or wood-based piece for hanging is finishing the sides. There are numerous ways you can do this. My favorite is to clean the edges on the palette and let the resulting swirl of absorbed pigment stand on its own. Leaving the edges unfinished works well if you're opting for a raw look, but there are also several ways to achieve a more polished presentation. Try the six options outlined on the following pages and pick the one you like best, or let them inspire other finishing techniques of your own.

> " A sincere artist is not
> one who makes a faithful
> attempt to put on to canvas
> what is in front of him,
> but one who tries to create
> something which is,
> in itself, a living thing. "
> **William Dobell**

87

WAX OFF

Before you finish your edges, you will want to remove the dripped wax from the wood. I must admit, however, that cleaning the wax off the edges and simply leaving the exposed wood is my finish of choice. It's easy and clean, and it gives neat, fresh edges to the painting. Regardless of your preference, if your painting dripped pigmented wax down the edges of your board, be aware that this technique tends to leave behind any color that was absorbed into the wood. If this bothers you, you'll definitely want to finish your edges with another method after you've removed the wax.

1

WHAT YOU'LL NEED

finished piece ✳ *hot palette* ✳ *paper towels*

Warm and remove wax

To remove the wax that has dripped down the side of the box, set it on the hot palette for a moment, then remove it and wipe the edge with a paper towel.

WAX ON

Simply waxing on the sides of the box is the easiest way to achieve a finished edge. If you decide to use this method, though, be aware that the wax can be fragile, and if it gets bumped or scratched it will come off and could damage the painting as well.

1

WHAT YOU'LL NEED

finished piece ✳ *wax* ✳ *paint in the color of your choosing*
heat gun or other fusing tool ✳ *paintbrush* ✳ *razor blade (optional)*

Remove drips and warm sides

Begin by using the Wax Off technique (above). Then, heat the sides of your board with a heat gun until they are warm to the touch.

2

Brush on tinted medium and fuse

Brush on a colored medium. If you apply too much, you can scrape away any excess with a razor blade. Fuse to finish.

PAINT

Painting the sides is simple, as well. Begin by using the Wax Off technique (see page 88). Then, you can use oil, acrylic, gouache, tempera or even latex house paints to finish your edges in the color of your choice.

1

WHAT YOU'LL NEED

finished piece ✳ *acrylic or other paint in a color of your choosing*
paintbrush

Paint edges

In this example I am using acrylic paint, but the same technique can be used for any type of paint. Since acrylic paints tend to be opaque, they are a great option for hiding any stains or drips on the raw wood. Simply paint a color that complements your finished piece onto the sides with your paintbrush of choice and allow it to dry.

STAIN

Finishing your edges by staining them achieves a transparent look that allows the wood grain to show through. Begin by using the Wax Off technique (see page 88). Then you can stain your edges using a color of ink that complements the colors in your finished piece, as shown here, or you can keep it real by opting for a natural wood stain finish.

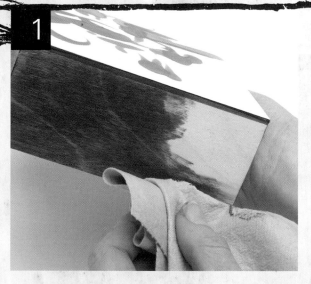

1

WHAT YOU'LL NEED

finished piece ✳ *ink or stain* ✳ *paper towels*
sandpaper or buffing tool (optional)

Apply ink or stain to sides

Apply ink or stain to a paper towel or other applicator of choice, then rub it over the box sides to stain the wood. (I'm using alcohol ink here, but any kind will do the job.) If a second coat is needed, sand or buff the surface before giving it a second coat.

SHELLAC

If you've taken on the shellac challenge and given it a try in encaustic (see page 76), then you have this on hand already. Apply it as you would a stain (see page 89). The main difference will be the shiny finish that results.

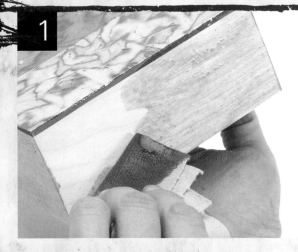

1

WHAT YOU'LL NEED

finished piece ✳ *shellac* ✳ *paper towels*

Use paper towel to apply shellac to clean edges

Be sure to remove all wax drips using the Wax Off technique (see page 88). Then, simply use a paper towel to coat the box sides with shellac.

FLOATER FRAME

Canvas floater frames are perfect for framing shallow-profile Claybord, flat panels and hardware store wood. They come ready-made at some framers, and most can create custom-made floaters, too.

1

WHAT YOU'LL NEED

finished piece ✳ *ready-made wooden floater frame of appropriate size* ✳ *4 L brackets*

Frame finished piece

Here I've chosen to display my piece in a ready-made wooden floater frame. First use L brackets to secure the painting in the frame, then use wire to hang it.

caring for your encaustic work

To care for your encaustic art, simply dust the surface with a feather duster or clean lint-free cloth. Occasional polishing with a clean, soft, untextured cloth will bring out depth and shine. Encaustic paintings should be shipped and stored in a temperature-controlled environment and should always be protected from extreme heat and freezing. Do not hang this or any art in direct sunlight. Any framing of encaustic prints should be done without the use of heat. Avoid contact of any glass portion of a frame with the surface.

HANGING WIRE

If you are familiar with using wire for hanging framed work, you'll find that wiring a cradled Claybord isn't all that different. In fact, cradled Claybords offer great profiles to hide the wiring within, allowing each painting to hang nice and flush on the wall.

1

WHAT YOU'LL NEED

finished piece ✳ *2 eye hooks or framing brackets length of wire, about twice the width of your Claybord drill (optional)*

Attach wire to insides of inner frame

Add a simple framing wire using eye hooks or framing brackets attached to the inside of the sides of the Claybord. If you're using eye hooks, predrill holes a quarter of the way from the top edge of your painting for best results.

GOT IT ALL

For this painting I combined the techniques of image transfer (see page 58), incising (see page 28) and scraping (see page 36), and enclosed the finished piece in a floater frame for display.

Get It
TOGETHER

Now that you've mastered a varied set of individual techniques, you're ready to start experimenting with combining them in different ways. The possibilities for creating a fluid, multitechnique encaustic painting are limitless.

This chapter will demonstrate this with a small selection of step by step projects to get you started. Not only will you learn how to create more advanced pieces, but you'll also learn how to combine the finished works to create a larger, more comprehensive unit with two multipiece projects: a diptych and a triptych. Finally, you'll find an inspiration gallery to further enliven your senses and inspire you to imaginative creativity in your own encaustic work. The rest is up to you!

> "The artist never entirely knows. We guess. We may be wrong, but we take leap after leap in the dark."
>
> **Agnes de Mille**

small scale

This is a quick, fun project for incorporating another piece of artwork into an encaustic work. It uses a portion of a watercolor painting as an underpainting to create depth of color under layers of medium. I then embellished the surface with a combination of techniques. You can try this approach to enhance any other types of works you've done; small collages, oil paintings and even colorful pastel drawings can become wonderful underpaintings.

WHAT YOU'LL NEED

5" × 5" × 2" (13cm × 13cm × 5cm) Claybord

medium

heat gun or other fusing tool

paintbrush

chipboard embellishments

other elements to imbed in wax

gold metallic leaf

oil paint stick or oil paint

watercolor painting or other collage paper of choice

gel medium

paper towels

rubber gloves

spoon or other burnishing tool

ball stylus (optional)

wire brush

Adhere underpainting

Choose an original watercolor or mixed-media work you'd like to use as a base/background for an encaustic painting. Begin by adhering the paper to the board using gel medium.

Layer medium

After the gel medium has dried completely, warm the board and begin applying wax medium, fusing between each layer. Continue until you've created an effect you like. I applied 4 layers of medium to add some depth.

Add texture

Once the medium has cooled, add texture to the outer edges of the surface with a wire brush.

techniques used

Heavyweight Paper (see page 46)
Found Objects (see page 50)
Rub-Ons (see page 62)
Metallic Leaf Transfers (see page 62)

Add oil paint to incised areas
Rub an oil paint stick (or regular oil paint) into the areas where you added texture with the wire brush.

Rub and remove excess paint
Wearing rubber gloves to protect your hands, work the paint thoroughly into all the grooves. Remove the excess paint with paper towel.

Add embellishments
Press the embellishments or additional elements of your choice into the wax. It is best to imbed items into warm wax, so if necessary, reheat the surface until it is warm. Re-fuse the surface.

Add wax to chipboard
Apply wax over the top of a few chipboard embellishments that you'd like to coat with foil and add to your piece in the following steps.

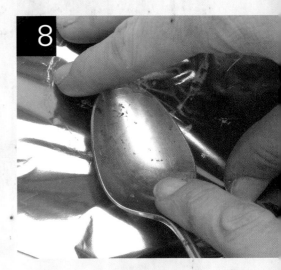

Burnish gold leaf
Use the back of a spoon to burnish a sheet of metallic leaf over the waxed chipboard embellishments.

Complete leaf transfer

Peel the leaf off to reveal the transfer and see if you wish to burnish any uncovered areas. Don't worry about covering the chipboard completely; it's okay if some of the original pattern on each piece shows through.

Adhere embellishments

If your chipboard pieces are self-adhesive, peel off the backing and stick them to the board. If they aren't self-adhesive, use a small amount of wax to adhere them.

Make adjustments and re-fuse

If you decide there is an element in your piece that isn't working, pop it off and simply re-fuse to erase the indentations in the wax. Here, I decided I didn't like the buttons, so I removed them.

Add finishing touches

Add any final touches. I used a ball stylus to impress dots of metallic leaf into the wax and to add some line work along the bottom for visual interest.

singular

Using an 8" × 8" × 2" (20cm × 20cm × 5cm) Claybord, I created this piece by combining some of my favorite techniques: sketching on Japanese silk tissue, oil glazing, incising, texturing and coffee ground inclusion. I love how the end result shows off the unique properties of the wax.

WHAT YOU'LL NEED

8" × 8" × 2"
(20cm × 20cm ×
5cm) Claybord

medium

heat gun or
other fusing tool

paintbrush

Japanese silk tissue

oil paint or oil paint stick

fine art marker

coffee grounds

incising tools

metal spoon

paper towels

razor blade

rubber gloves

linseed oil (optional)

1

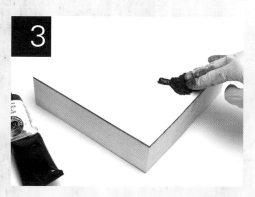

Create sketch
Create a small doodle or drawing on a square of Japanese silk tissue paper. I am using a permanent marker, but you can use any art medium you choose.

2

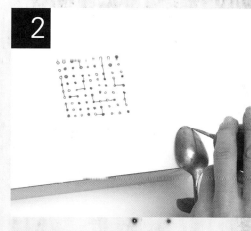

Add medium, fuse and incise
Brush one layer of medium over the surface to prime it, and fuse. Let it cool. Set the drawing on a cool, primed board to establish its placement. Then, add incising lines around the edges by tracing around the bowl of a spoon.

3

Add oil paint
Remove the tissue-paper drawing from the board. Squeeze out a small amount of oil paint and wearing gloves, work it into the incised areas.

techniques used
Tissue Paper (see page 42)
Incising (see page 28)

Troubleshoot any oil stains

Rub off any excess oil. If some remains on the wax, use a bit of linseed oil to take it off all the way back to just the incised lines. (Make certain that you remove all the oil afterward, or it will cause the next layer of wax to resist adhesion.)

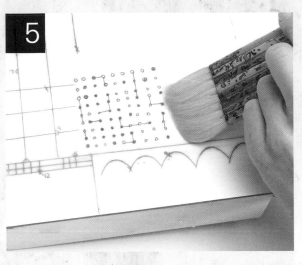

Adhere drawing

Use clear medium to adhere the tissue drawing in the position you determined in step 2.

Layer medium and fuse

Brush one layer over the tissue and re-fuse. Then, build up several layers of medium on the board, working around the tissue to sort of frame it in with a thicker surrounding area of medium, re-fusing between layers.

Add coffee grounds to frame area

Once you've created the depth of "frame" you desire, sprinkle coffee grounds onto the still warm wax.

Carefully fuse coffee grounds

Fuse the grounds to set them into the wax. Use a gentle airflow to control the wax melt and to keep the grounds from blowing away.

Incise to define frame

Once the wax has cooled, give the frame area more definition by running a razor blade along the edges.

Add oil paint to incised area

Lightly rub on a small amount of oil stick, just around the perimeter of the defined frame line.

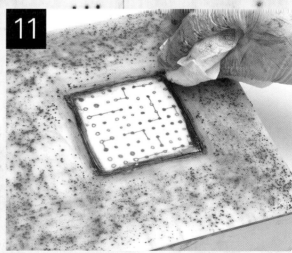

Remove excess and re-fuse

With a paper towel, gently remove the excess paint. Re-fuse to complete.

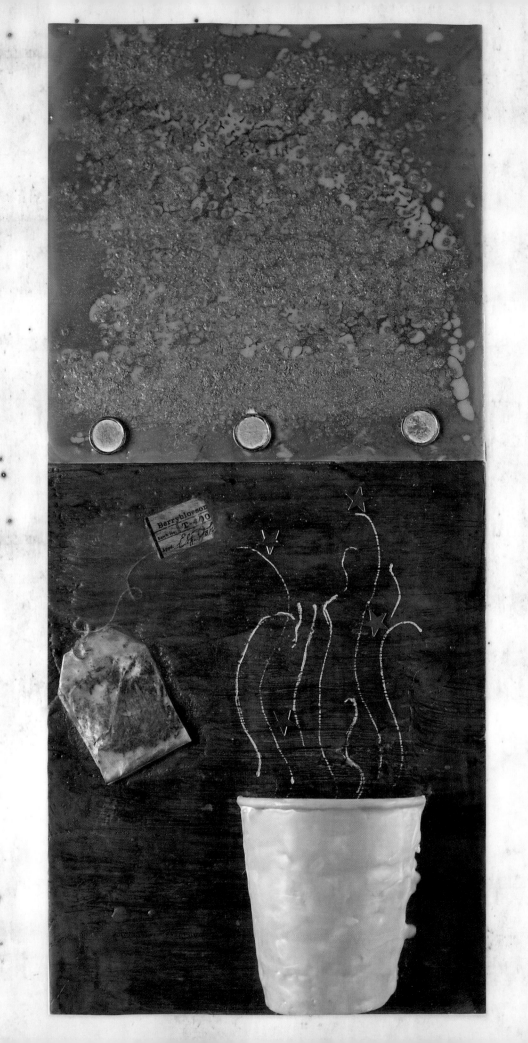

diptych

A diptych is a painting that combines two separate works to suggest the look of one. The individual pieces are either literally connected, as with this project, or simply designed to be displayed side by side. The beauty of using these Claybords is that Ampersand takes custom orders, making it a blast for you to use in endlessly varying sizes and combinations. For this diptych, I'm using 8" × 8" (20cm × 20cm) and 8" ×10" (20cm × 25cm) Claybords. The piece comes together playfully and uniquely to show off the versatility of the format.

WHAT YOU'LL NEED

8" × 10" (20cm × 25cm) Claybord

8" × 8" (20cm × 20cm) Claybord

medium

heat gun or other fusing tool

paintbrush

patterned paper

King's Blue wax paint (R&F)

mica powder

black oil paint stick

paper coffee cup

silver star-shaped stickers or other embellishments

tea bag, unused and dry

white wax paint

gel medium

wood glue

matches or butane torch

paper towels

razor blade

rubber gloves

scissors or craft knife

shellac

stylus

white transfer paper

fine-grit sandpaper (optional)

Adhere paper to first board

Use gel medium to adhere a piece of patterned paper to a clean 8" × 10" (20cm × 25cm) board. Smooth the paper down, being careful not to get any gel medium on top of the paper. Let it dry. Then, trim off the excess paper using a razor blade.

Sand paper if desired, then apply medium

If your paper has a gloss to it that may resist wax, eliminate it with a quick sanding with a fine-grit sandpaper. Apply a coat or two of wax medium, applying the wax in a textured application. Fuse between each layer.

techniques used

Heavyweight Paper (see page 46)

Found Objects (see page 50)

Rub-Ons (see page 62)

Shellac (see page 76)

Mica Powder (see page 77)

Add black oil paint
Wearing rubber gloves to protect your hands, rub a black oil paint stick over the surface of the papered, primed board. Where you applied the medium texturally with visible brushstrokes, the oil paint should be picked up in an interesting, similarly textured appearance.

Remove excess oil paint
Use a paper towel to remove excess oil paint.

Add and paint tea bag
Use a puddle of clear medium to adhere a tea bag to the surface. Using the same paper towel you used to remove the black paint, rub just a bit over the bag and the tag to incorporate them into the background, then rub off the excess.

Coat cup with colored wax
Use scissors or a craft knife to cut the coffee cup in half vertically. If it isn't already plain white, coat one half of it with white encaustic paint first to prime it. Then, paint it with wax tinted with Kings Blue. Let it dry.

Add cup to composition
Set this cup onto the board, add a bit of clear medium to adhere it securely to the surface, and fuse.

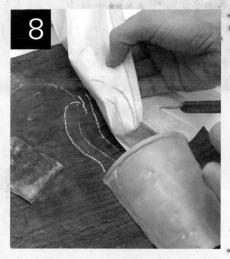

Create steam lines

Positioning the white transfer paper over the cup, use a stylus to draw decorative lines of steam.

Add star embellishments

Push a few silver stars or other embellishments into the wax surface to add interest.

Begin second board

Prime the 8" × 8" (20cm × 20cm) board. Apply a layer or two of King's Blue encaustic paint.

Apply shellac

Over the surface of the blue board, dab on a coat of shellac.

Add mica powder

Sprinkle silver mica powder into the wet shellac. Light the shellac on fire with a match or butane torch. Allow the shellac to burn until it goes out on its own. Add any additional elements you'd like to the surface to complete this piece. (I added just a few paper buttons to enhance the composition.)

Assemble and adhere pieces

Use wood glue to adhere the boards together just as you did with the triptych (see page 101).

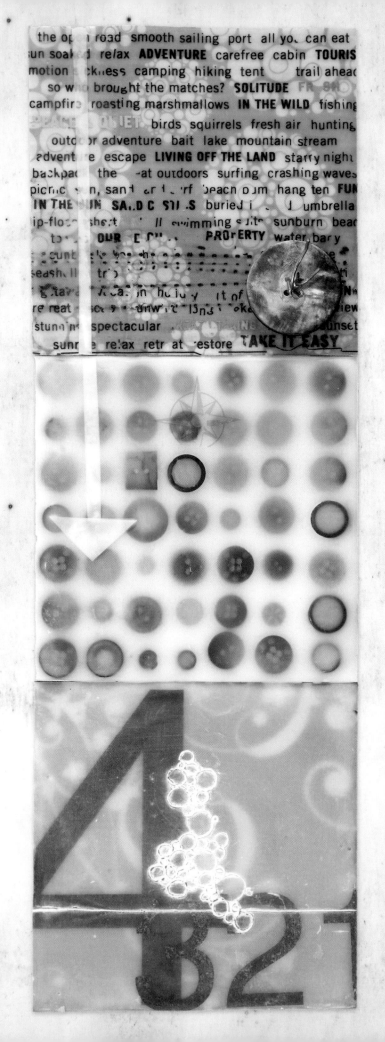

triptych

A triptych employs the same principle as the diptych, only using three panels instead of two. Here I am combining different techniques in interesting ways—using embedded objects, oil bar glazing, image transfer, rub-ons and collage—to pull three 5" × 5" (13cm × 13cm) Claybords together as a unified piece.

WHAT YOU'LL NEED

5" × 5" (13cm × 13cm) primed Claybords, 3

medium

heat gun or other fusing tool

paintbrush

buttons or other embellishments

patterned paper

oil paints

oil paint sticks

rub-ons

texture-making tools (a straight pin and a perforation tool are used here)

toner or laser photocopies of numbers and/or any other imagery

gel medium

rubber gloves

paper towels

razor blade

sandpaper

scissors

spoon or burnishing tool

water

wood glue

Imbed elements in first board

Start with a primed board and lay your elements, such as the buttons I am using here, into the warm surface. When the elements are arranged to your liking, drizzle clear medium over them. Fuse. If you want to achieve a smooth finish around the elements, you'll want to overfuse. Here I applied several layers of medium, fusing between each, in order to level the wax with the elements. Let it cure. (While you are waiting, feel free to skip to step 3 and return to step 2 later.)

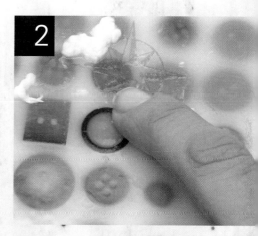

Add image transfer

Once your piece has cured, enhance the depth of the piece by adding an image to the surface layer of wax. Here I placed a photocopied image of a compass rose and transferred it into the wax.

techniques used

Incising (see page 28)
Tissue Paper (see page 42)
Heavyweight Paper (see page 46)
Found Objects (see page 50)
Image Transfers (see page 58)
Rub-Ons (see page 62)
Finishing Sides (see page 86)

Adhere paper to second board

Adhere patterned paper to what will be the second board of your triptych with gel medium. Smooth the paper to remove any bubbles, but be careful not to let any gel medium ooze onto the top of the paper, or it will act as a resist. Let it dry completely. (You can also adhere it with wax instead, if you wish.)

Trim paper flush with board

Trim the excess paper from the edges of the board with a razor blade.

Prime and fuse surface

Paint a layer of encaustic medium over the paper. Treat this first layer as the priming layer, and fuse it smooth to ensure additional layers will have a level base.

Layer medium thickly

Continue adding medium layers to the papered board, fusing between layers.

Continue until desired effect is reached

Work in this manner until the look of the paper is diffused by the thick medium. Five layers created the nice, muted, dimensional effect shown here. Let it cure. (Feel free to skip to step 15 while you wait, returning to steps 8–14 later.)

Create embellishment for second board

Print an image from your computer that you would like to feature on your piece. If it's a number or a letter, like I chose here, be sure to print it in reverse so that when it is transferred the image will be accurate. Cut it out with scissors.

Begin image transfer

Heat the surface of the board, then set the photocopy facedown into the wax. Burnish it with a spoon, being sure to rub every bit of the image. Pour a small amount of water onto the paper. Let it absorb.

Complete transfer

Burnish the back of the wet copy with the spoon once again. Once the paper begins to pulp, use your fingers to rub away the paper and reveal the transfer.

Fuse, add medium and transfer second image

Re-fuse the transfer layer. Apply one coat of clear medium over the transfer, then repeat steps 8–10 with a second image to make a second transfer over that layer. Repeat this to add as many layers of transfers as you'd like.

Incise surface

Incise a design into the top layer using a metal tool with a fine tip. (Here I'm using a straight pin to create a series of small circles and a line.)

Apply oil paint to incised area

Wearing rubber gloves to protect your hands, apply oil paint in the color of your choice over the area you incised in the previous step. Here I'm using Titanium White.

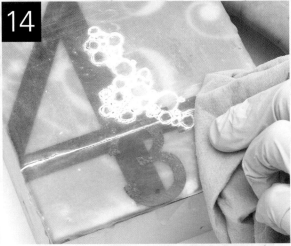

Work paint into marks and remove excess

Work the paint thoroughly into the incising. Remove the excess with a paper towel.

15

Begin third board

Begin the third board by repeating steps 3–5 using a different patterned paper. You can go on to repeat steps 6–7 to tone down the look of the paper, or leave the medium at just one layer, as I did here. Let the surface cure. Then, burnish a rub-on transfer of your choice over the surface.

16

Add texture

Add some texture lines with a perforation tool or another tool of your choice. Or, if you prefer, you can incise the surface free-hand as in step 12.

17

Add oil paint to impressions in medium

Rub an oil stick over the incised area, or apply oil paint straight from the tube if you prefer.

18

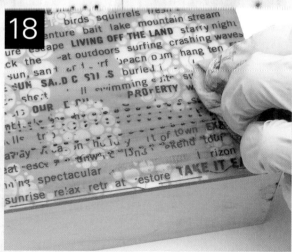

Work paint into marks and remove excess

Work the paint thoroughly into the incised area. Then, rub the excess paint off with a paper towel.

Prepare to add final embellishment

Decide where you'd like to add an object to the composition of this board, and apply a puddle of wax to that area. Here I've decided to add a large button in the lower right-hand corner.

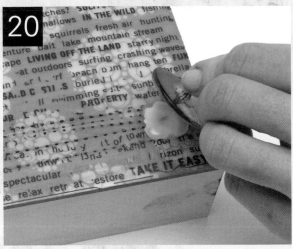

Adhere embellishment and fuse

Gently press the button in the warm puddle of wax so it will adhere completely. Fuse it gently and allow the surface to cool completely.

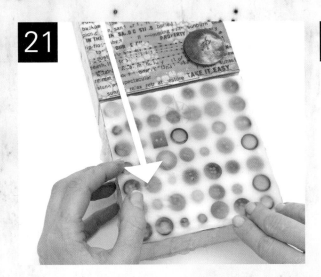

Align boards and overlap embelishment

Align the first and second boards for the triptych. Use a rub-on embellishment, such as this arrow, to overlap both boards and tie the composition together. Burnish it into place on both boards.

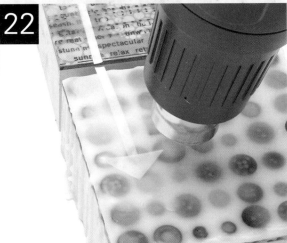

Cut embellishment, add medium and fuse

Using a razor blade, cut the arrow at the joint of the two boards. Brush clear medium over both boards, and fuse them.

Remove wax from sides

On the edges of all three boards where they will meet, clean the sides by heating them on the warm palette and wiping clean with a paper towel (see page 88). Then, sand them to remove any remaining wax residue and ensure good adhesion when the triptych is assembled.

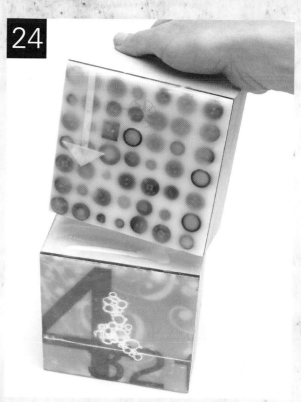

Assemble and adhere triptych

Apply wood glue to the first side, then stack the second on top of it. Repeat for the third and set the whole triptych aside to dry. Finish the edges any way you'd like (see pages 88–90), or not at all.

brush up

When combining techniques, don't set too many rules for yourself to follow. The more layers of wax you apply, the less the initial layering or techniques will become evident—so if you don't like the look of something, you can simply cover it with additional layers.

inspiration GALLERY

"Always be a first-rate version of yourself,
instead of a second-rate version of somebody else." **Judy Garland**

The encaustic paintings on the following pages exemplify just a few more of
the many ways you can combine, showcase and reinvent the techniques you've
learned throughout this book. I hope they inspire you to take your work in new
creative directions in your own encaustic workshop.

GIRLS RULE

Eco-Fashion
Comes of Age

THE
LOCAL

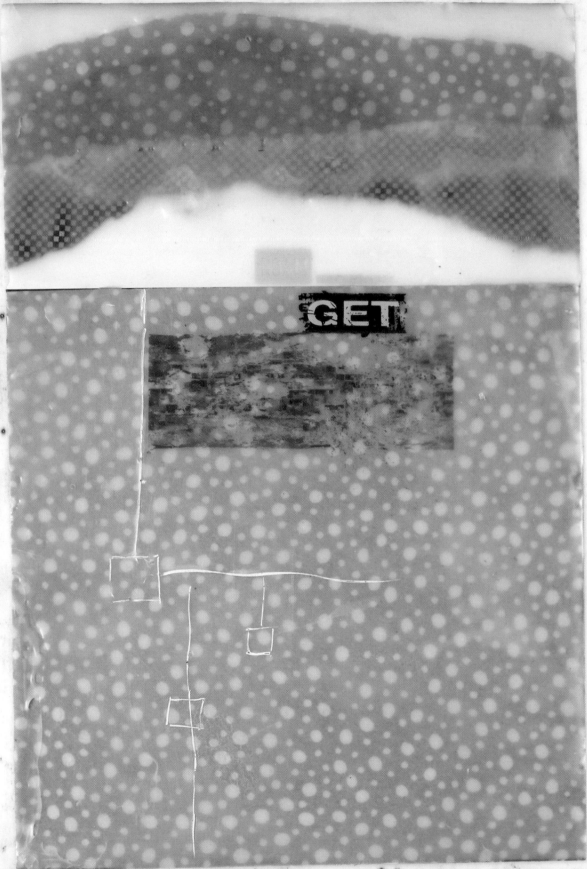

GET

GONE

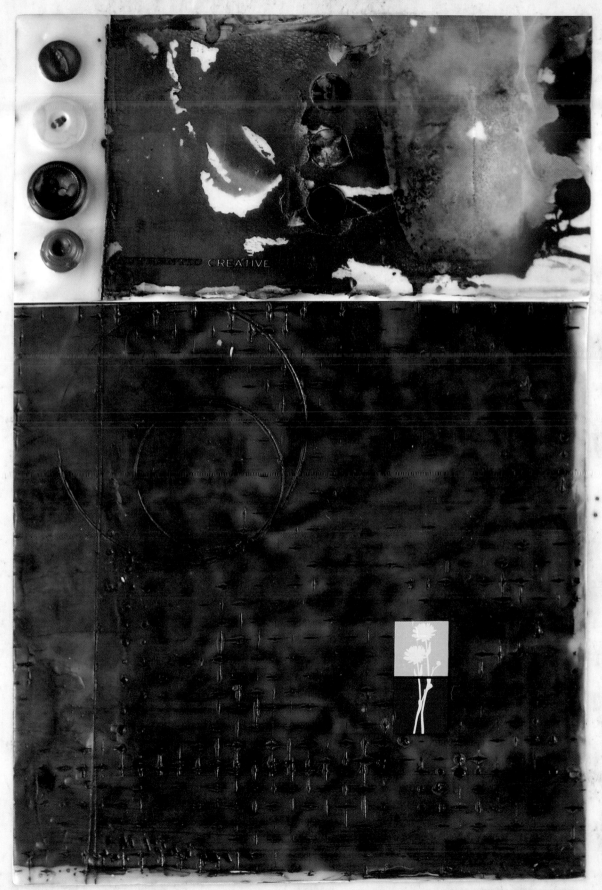

CREATIVE

AUTHENTIC YOU

SO

118

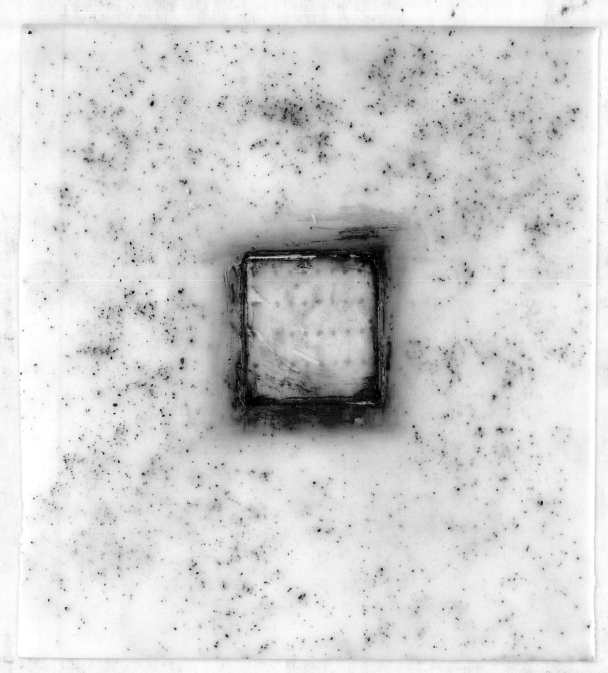

COFFEE TIME

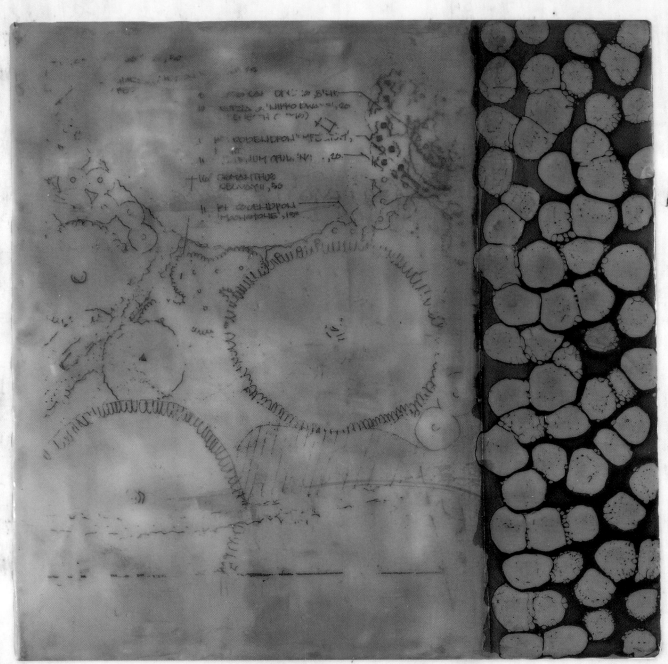

TREED

LONGTIME COMING

SPRING CITY

SUNRISE

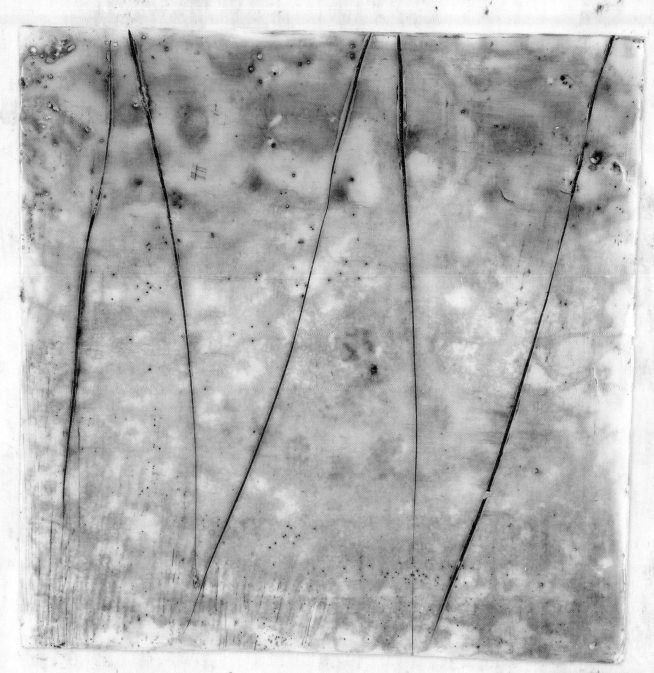

SUNSET

RESOURCES

Each of us is here with a reason; each of us with something to make. If you haven't gathered through reading this book, I have some very favorite sources for my encaustic and general art supplies. Visit these Web sites or, if you are lucky enough, the actual, physical stores, for everything you need to create a look of your own. And, of course, make sure you visit your local craft store with new eyes for inspiration. Other great sources for both supplies and ideas include pottery stores, book-binding stores, thrift stores and flea markets.

R&F Handmade Paints
www.rfpaints.com
encaustic paints and more

Daniel Smith Art Materials
www.danielsmith.com
Claybords, mediums, palettes, ink cans and more

International Encaustic Artists
www.international-encaustic-artists.org
support and community of like-minded souls

Ampersand Art Supply
www.ampersandart.com
(custom orders and product information only; boards available through Daniel Smith Art Materials)

Fine Art Store
www.fineartstore.com
800-836-8940
Encaustsikos! Wax Paints and Tools

ABOUT PATRICIA

The most important thing in my life, and the most valuable job I've ever had, is being a mom. My four boys are my greatest creation and my life's purpose. They are all redheaded teenagers now, each one unique and each one invaluable. I became a mom at twenty-three and haven't looked back.

I keep food in the cupboards for these rapidly growing boys through my painting: selling it, teaching it, demoing it and writing about it. Enjoy what you have and pass it on!

I have been painting and creating all my life but have no formal training, other than a B.S. in English from the University of Colorado. I invented myself as an artist by way of workshops throughout the United States. I feel fortunate in having come to art by following this path because I've never had anyone tell me I "can't do that," and have tried it all. Passion persuades!

Encaustic came my way about seven years ago when I began experimenting with hot wax in my mixed-media work. Deciding I needed to find out how to "really" use it, I took a workshop through

R&F Handmade Paints and have been hooked ever since! In fact, I'd highly recommend everyone take a workshop in this medium. Even if this book carries you along as I hope it will, a workshop is an invaluable experience not to be missed. Choose a local workshop, or come to one of mine! You can find out more about my encaustic classes at www.pbsartist.com.

I will never grow tired of this medium, as it offers neverending possibilities in experimentation and discovery. I continue to work in water media and collage on paper and canvas in between throwing hot wax about.

INDEX

Wax artistic WITH THESE OTHER INSPIRING NORTH LIGHT BOOKS.

Taking Flight
by Kelly Rae Roberts

In *Taking Flight*, you'll find inspiration to grow your creative wings. You'll learn the mixed-media painting techniques Kelly Rae Roberts employs to create her artwork, including layering paints and incorporating meaningful phrases. Then follow prompts to begin your own creative journey—look for the sacred in the ordinary and embrace your innermost fears, then incorporate what you find into your art. Take further inspiration from the gallery projects by the author and contributors, then spread your artistic wings and make art of your own.

ISBN 13: 978-1-60061-082-0
ISBN 10: 1-60061-082-X
paperback, 128 pages, Z1930

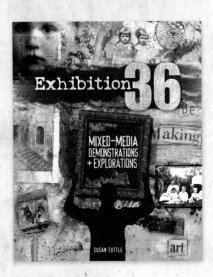

Exhibition 36
by Susan Tuttle

Inside *Exhibition 36*, you'll enter a virtual gallery featuring the work of thirty-six mixed-media artists, including Claudine Hellmuth, Suzanne Simanaitis and Kelly Moore. Wander through the virtual exhibits and take inspiration from collage, digital art, assemblage, and altered and repurposed artwork. Each artist is "present" in his or her exhibit, answering questions, sharing thoughts, talking about the work and offering instruction. You'll get insight into the artists' creative processes and be inspired by the articles, techniques and artwork they share. As a bonus, you'll find imagery contributed by the artists for you to reuse in your own creations.

ISBN-13: 978-1-60061-104-9
ISBN-10: 1-60061-104-4
paperback, 160 pages, Z2065

Rethinking Acrylic
by Patti Brady

Rethinking Acrylic offers you radical solutions for using the world's most versatile medium. Acrylic paint can mimic oil paint, watercolor, gouache and encaustic; it can be applied in subtle washes, or troweled as thick as impasto; it can be as transparent as glass or as dense and as dark as tar. You'll get an in-depth approach to the most popular techniques with twenty-seven mini-demonstrations and thirty-five full demonstrations that show you how to incorporate featured techniques into completed paintings.

ISBN 13: 978-1-60061-013-4
ISBN 10: 1-60061-013-7
hardcover, 160 pages, Z1060

These and other fine North Light Books are available at your local craft retailer, bookstore or online supplier, or visit our Web site at **www.mycraftivity.com**.